●●●●●● **THIS**

citizenship

1

THIS IS...
citizenship

1

TERRY FIEHN

JOHN MURRAY

Key words are defined in the list on page 113.

First published 2002
by John Murray (Publishers) Ltd
50 Albemarle Street
London W1S 4BD

Reprinted 2002 (twice)

Layouts by Jenny Fleet
Artwork by Art Construction, Karen Donnelly, Richard Duszczak, Peter Greenwood,
    Chris Pavely, Steve Smith
Typeset in Bodoni Book by Wearset, Boldon, Tyne and Wear
Colour separations by Colourscript, Mildenhall, Suffolk
Printed and bound in Spain by Bookprint, S. L., Barcelona

A catalogue entry for this title is available from the British Library.

ISBN 0 7195 7719 5
Teacher's Resource Book 0 7195 7720 9

Contents

Acknowledgements

The authors are particularly grateful to Maqsood Ahmad and Samantha Corbin for allowing us to use their experiences of racism in Section 2.

Photographs reproduced by kind permission of:
Cover Image State; **p.22** With permission of Maqsood Ahmad; **p.23** With permission of Samantha Corbin; **pp.25–26** 'Show Racism the Red Card'; **p.27** *tl* © Stu Forster/AllSport, *tr* Chelsea Ladies Football Club, *bl* © Tony O'Brien/AllSport; **p.31** © Robert Gibbs/Impact; **p.32** Scope; **p56** *Bucks Free Press*, 4 August 2000; **p.72** With permission of Jenny Tonge; **p.80** With permission of Mercury One2One; **p.81** *t* With permission of Ball Park Franks, *b* With permission of TEAC; **p.82** With permission of TCB, Alberto; **p.85** Alban Donohoe Picture Service; **p.86** Richard Stonehouse/Camera Press; **p.87** *t* Toby Melville, The Press Association Ltd, *b* Paul Faith, The Press Association Ltd; **p.88** Paul Faith, The Press Association Ltd; **p.89** © Camera Press Digital; **p.98** *tl* Hartmut Schwarzbach/Still Pictures, *tr* Bikas Das/Associated Press, *br* Ron Giling/Still Pictures, *bl* European Press Agency, The Press Association Ltd; **p.99** *tl* Hartmut Schwarzbach/Still Pictures, *tr* Ron Giling/Still Pictures, *br* Mark Edwards/Still Pictures, *bl* Hartmut Schwarzbach/Still Pictures; **p.101** © Mian Khursheed/Reuters/Popperfoto; **p.102** © STR/Reuters/Popperfoto; **p.103** © Simon Denyer/STR/Reuters/Popperfoto; **p.104** Ricardo Mazalan/Associated Press; **p.107** From 'Everybody has a Basic Right to ...' reproduced with permission of Oxfam Publishing, 274 Banbury Road, Oxford, OX2 7DZ; **p.109** 'h₂0p to it!' reproduced with permission of Water Aid, London, SE1 7UB; **p.111** *t* Mark Lennihan/Associated Press, *m* Sayyid Azim/Associated Press, *b* Joel Rubin/Associated Press.

t = top, *m* = middle, *b* = bottom, *r* = right, *l* = left

Text extracts reproduced by kind permission of:
pp.4–5 Extract from *The Demon Headmaster* by Gillian Cross, by permission of Oxford University Press; **pp.26–27** Interviews reproduced with permission of 'Kick it Out', Unit 3, 1–4 Christina Street, London, EC2A 4PA; **pp.30–31** With permission of 'Street Child Africa'; **p.31** Chris Holt, CAFOD; **p.32** Scope; **p.37** 'No Room for Racism' from the Commission for Racial Equality; **p.38** 'Show Racism the Red Card'; **p.56** 'Row kicks off over stadium's yes vote' from the *Wandsworth Borough Guardian*, 8 March 2001, 'Scrawlers could be forced to wear pink' from the *Richmond Informer*, 28 April 2000, 'Meet Violet the kung fu rabbit' from the *Bucks Free Press*, 4 August 2000; **p.57** 'End of the line for our rail users?' from the *Cornish Guardian*, 10 August 2000, Bodmin, 'All change to homes and shops at Leadmill' from the *Sheffield Telegraph*, 1 September 2001; **p.85** © News International Newspapers Limited (March 29 2000).

section 1

Rules, fairness and participation
What makes rules fair?

Key words
- rules
- fairness
- punishment
- sanction

When people live together in groups, they need to obey rules if they are to get on with each other. If people did exactly as they wanted all the time, others would suffer. For example, there are rules saying you cannot steal things and rules saying you cannot hurt other people. These rules are designed to prevent arguments and fights developing. However, it can sometimes be difficult to apply rules fairly.

In this section, you will learn about:

* the need for rules in social groups
* the way rules are made
* what happens when rules are broken
* what fairness is
* school and class rules
* how you can set up or improve your school council.

You will:

* find out about your school's rules
* discuss your school's rules in small groups and with the whole class
* make decisions
* give your opinion and explain it to others
* think about and understand other people's opinions.

Planet Hoff wants to join the United Council for Galactic Trade. However, before it can join, it has to satisfy the rules of the United Council. You are a member of the United Council's visiting team of investigators. The team is looking at every aspect of life on Hoff. Your job is to investigate how schools are run and whether rules are fair to pupils.

You can find out more about Planet Hoff on pages 18–19, 62–63 and 90–91.

People at Zap High School

There are four groups of people in Zap High School:

Knowers pass on their knowledge and skills to the Learners. They do not discipline the Learners.

Enforcers do not teach. They punish anyone who misbehaves in class or breaks the school rules. They keep records on the Learners based on reports sent to them by the Knowers. The Learners are not allowed to see these records.

Learners are the school students.

Monitors are a small group of senior Learners specially chosen and trained by the Enforcers. The Monitors do this work in secret. Only the Enforcers know who they are.

Rules and punishments at Zap High School

Zap High School is very strict. There are very clear rules which were made many years ago when the school was founded. Changes to the rules are never allowed, or even discussed. The rules are pinned on the walls of the school and are sent to every family when a student joins the school.

Punishments for breaking the rules are worked out on a points system. For example, talking in class has a score of 4 points, and rudeness to a Knower is worth 10 points. If a Learner talks in class **and** is rude, the punishment is worth 14 points. This points system is also pinned on the walls of the school and sent to Learners' homes. Here are some of the rules and punishments:

Rules	Points
Leaving doors open, leaving taps running	1
Dropping litter, running	2
Arriving late to class	3
Talking in class	4
Chewing, eating	5
Swearing	6
Rudeness to Knower	10

Points	Punishments
1	Standing still in middle of dining hall for 10 minutes during lunch
2	Writing 50 lines
3	Detention for 30 minutes after school
4	Letter home and detention for one hour
5	One stroke of cane on hand
10	Five strokes of cane on hand

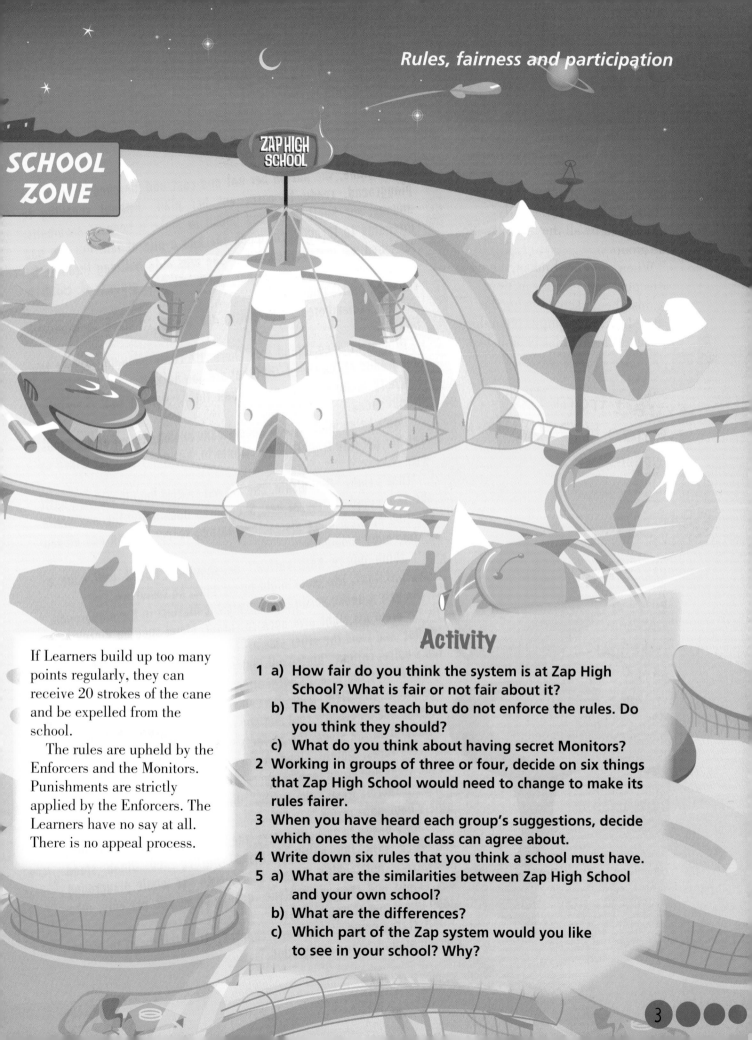

SCHOOL ZONE

ZAP HIGH SCHOOL

If Learners build up too many points regularly, they can receive 20 strokes of the cane and be expelled from the school.

The rules are upheld by the Enforcers and the Monitors. Punishments are strictly applied by the Enforcers. The Learners have no say at all. There is no appeal process.

Activity

1 a) How fair do you think the system is at Zap High School? What is fair or not fair about it?

b) The Knowers teach but do not enforce the rules. Do you think they should?

c) What do you think about having secret Monitors?

2 Working in groups of three or four, decide on six things that Zap High School would need to change to make its rules fairer.

3 When you have heard each group's suggestions, decide which ones the whole class can agree about.

4 Write down six rules that you think a school must have.

5 a) What are the similarities between Zap High School and your own school?

b) What are the differences?

c) Which part of the Zap system would you like to see in your school? Why?

1.2 Whose rules?

All groups of people develop rules, whether the group is a family, a group of friends, a youth club or a school. Some of the rules are formal and written down. Others are informal, but are still clearly understood by all the members of the group.

When rules are broken, the group uses punishments, or sanctions, against the person breaking the rules. In schools, pupils often think they have been unfairly punished.

Extract from *The Demon Headmaster*
by Gillian Cross

At playtime, she put on her hat and coat and marched out into the playground, ready to carry out her plan. Without speaking to anyone, she knelt down and began to make a heap of snowballs, intending to throw them when she had a pile of ten. But she had reckoned without Harvey. When she was only halfway through, he came bounding across to her, past all the groups of children chanting tables and dates ...

'You remembered. We really *are* going to have a snowball fight!' ...

Almost at once, Lloyd was there. He came bounding across the playground at top speed. 'H! What are you doing?'

'We're going to have a snowball fight,' Harvey said cheerfully. 'It's Di's idea.'

'Don't be an idiot.' Lloyd knocked the snowballs out of his hands. 'Let her get into trouble if she wants to, but don't you get mixed up with it.'

'That's right,' Dinah said. She did not realise how it sounded until she saw Lloyd staring at her. She stared back defiantly, and while the two of them were distracted, Harvey scooped down and picked up two more snowballs.

'I think you're both rotten!' he shouted. 'And I *will* have a snowball fight. The snow might be all gone, by tomorrow.'

His yell sounded eerily loud among the mutters in the playground. As he drew his right arm back to throw, Lloyd shouted warningly, 'H! No!' and from the other side of the playground came the sound of Ian's voice, calling, 'Watch out, you lot!'

But it was too late. As total silence fell over the playground, the two snowballs flew from Harvey's gloved hands and spattered messily, one on Lloyd's coat and one on Dinah's.

Ranged on the steps, the prefects were staring at them, a row of six stern faces. Slowly, Lloyd, Harvey and Dinah walked to the foot of the steps and stood looking up.

'Wait there!' Rose said curtly. 'We'll deal with you when the others have gone inside.'

As Rose began to call out orders, the neat rows of children formed and filed into the building. Lloyd, Harvey and Dinah stood awkwardly, not looking at each other, until the whole playground was empty and they were alone, gazing up at the prefects, who stood like a row of iron statues.

Jeff stared down at them and chanted, 'It is forbidden to waste time by playing in the playground.'

'It is forbidden,' Rose went on, 'to make a mess of your school uniform.'

'You must be punished,' Sarah said.

'In a suitable manner,' finished off Simon, smiling slightly.

Drawing together, the prefects whispered for a moment and then Rose turned to them again. 'Go inside,' she rapped out. 'Take off your hats and coats and gloves. Then come back here.'

As they walked towards the cloakroom, Dinah whispered to Lloyd, 'What will happen? What will they do?'

'I don't know,' he said sourly. 'But whatever it is, it'll be all your fault. I wish you'd never come.'

'No, it's my fault,' Harvey said in a miserable voice. 'I threw the snowballs. And whatever they do, it'll be *terrible*.'

When they came out of the door again, four of the prefects had gone. Rose was standing looking out over the playground, with a pleased smile on her face, and Jeff was by her side, holding three long-handled brooms.

'Now,' he said in a silky voice, 'you're very lucky. We've decided to be kind to you.' Lloyd and Harvey looked uneasily at each other.

'Yes.' Rose's smile broadened. 'Because you're so fond of playing with the snow, we're going to let you have some more of it.'

Jeff held out the brooms. 'You will each take one of these, and you will sweep all the snow from the playground into a heap. Then,' he looked at Rose, with a grin, 'you will make the whole heap into a pile of snowballs.'

For a second, Harvey looked perplexed, but Lloyd burst out, 'Aren't you going to let us put on our coats and things?'

Rose went on smiling. 'Certainly not.'

'But you can't do that! Harvey's got a weak chest. He could be ill. He...'

'Silence!'

'Suppose we say no?' asked Dinah, in a stiff voice.

Rose and Jeff looked at her as if she had said something unbelievably stupid.

Together, they chanted, 'The prefects are the voice of the Headmaster. They must be obeyed.'

Then Jeff thrust the brooms at them. 'Get sweeping!'

Resigned, Lloyd and Harvey trailed off down the steps, dragging their brooms after them. Dinah lingered rebelliously for a second or two, then joined them at the far end of the playground.

'Let's do it as quickly as we can,' she said. 'Perhaps that'll keep us warm.'

Discuss

1 Was the punishment unfair?

2 Were the rules in the Demon Headmaster's school unreasonable?

3 Which of these two statements do you agree with?
   a) 'Rules should never be broken.'
   b) 'There are times when you have to break rules.'

School rules

Schools usually have formal, written rules, which aim to keep order and protect the rights of everyone in the school.

1 a) Work alone or with pupils who went to the same primary school as you. Write down as many rules from your primary school as you can remember.

b) Which rules do you think were essential? Which rules were not essential? Underline essential rules in one colour and non-essential rules in another.

2 a) Compare your rules with those from other primary schools. How similar are the sets of rules?

b) With the rest of the class, agree which rules you think all primary schools should have.

3 In groups, look at the secondary school rules given to you by your teacher. Decide which of the rules you would change if you could. Then justify your choice to the rest of the class.

5 a) How are rules made in friendship groups?

b) What happens when somebody breaks the rules of the friendship group?

c) Is the treatment they receive always fair?

d) What happens when one of your friends is bullied by other pupils?

e) What happens when one of your friends bullies someone else?

4 a) Who makes rules in schools?

b) What happens if rules are broken in schools?

c) Should everyone be involved in making school rules?

6 a) Work in pairs. One of you is 'X', the other is 'Y'.

- X writes the beginning of a story in which a rule is broken. Don't tell Y what you are writing.
- Y writes the end of a story which tells about how somebody is punished after he or she has broken a rule.
- X and Y swap stories.
- X writes the beginning of Y's story. Y writes the end of X's story.

b) Choose some of the stories to read out in class.

Making your own class rules

Each class is part of the school, and so everyone in it must obey the school rules. But each class could also develop its own rules about how people work together.

7 Working in pairs, use the statement starters on the right to draw up your own rules for your class.

8 When you have finished, join up with another pair and share what you have written. Try to agree a final rule for each statement. You can add any others that you think are important.

9 All the fours should then come together as a class and agree a set of rules. Make posters of the agreed rules to display around the class.

Statement starters

A 'When we are discussing as a class, we should …'

B 'When someone is talking, we should …'

C 'If someone disagrees with what someone else has said, …'

D 'If there are different views in the class, we could …'

E 'Decisions could be made by …'

F 'If we don't understand what someone has said, we should …'

G 'If someone breaks the rules, …'

H 'If someone is unkind, …'

1.3 It's not fair!

Young children often say 'It's not fair!' when they mean 'It's not what I want.' It is important to understand what fairness is. Most of us like to think that we are fair to other people, and we want to be treated fairly ourselves.

Some people would say that, in order to be fair, we must:

* treat people equally
* not favour particular people
* not discriminate against particular people
* be open-minded and consider all the facts and viewpoints before coming to a decision
* be sure that punishments are not too harsh or too lenient.

The trouble is that it is not always easy to judge what is fair, as you can see from the cartoon strip 'Sam's Bad Day'.

Activity

1 **Read the cartoon strip. Then answer these questions with a partner.**
   a) **What do you think of each of the things that happened to Sam?**
   b) **Were the punishments fair?**
   c) **Who was at fault, if anyone?**
   d) **What could Sam do?**
2 **Look again at the list of ways of being fair above. Would you add anything else to the list?**
3 **Now discuss the same questions as a class.**

Sam's Bad Day

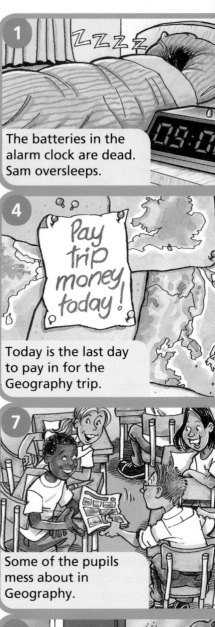

1 The batteries in the alarm clock are dead. Sam oversleeps.

4 Today is the last day to pay in for the Geography trip.

7 Some of the pupils mess about in Geography.

10 Sam arrives home. It's been a very bad day. Can it get worse?

2

Sam misses the bus and drops some money.

3

The teacher takes Sam's name. Detention tomorrow.

FAIR OR UNFAIR?

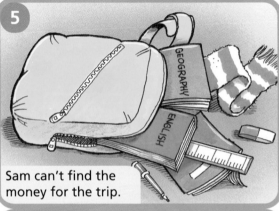

5

Sam can't find the money for the trip.

6

I'm sorry. If you haven't got the money today, you can't go on the trip.

Sam can't go on the trip.

FAIR OR UNFAIR?

8

The teacher keeps the whole class in for break. Sam misses the drama meeting.

9

Sam can't be in the drama production. All the parts have gone.

I'm sorry. All the parts are gone. You're too late.

FAIR OR UNFAIR?

11

Mum wants Sam to pick up the baby tomorrow, but Sam can't because of the detention.

12

Sam is grounded for getting three detentions this month.

FAIR OR UNFAIR?

Who will go to the TV studio?

Being fair is never easy. How would you reach a fair decision in the following example?

The problem

A class has entered a national competition. The competition involved everyone writing stories and doing paintings on the theme of 'Reducing Waste'. The whole class put together a folder on their project and it was sent off to the competition organisers. The prize is a visit to a TV studio where their work will be shown on television.

Excellent news! The class has been invited to the TV studio along with several other schools to show their work on waste reduction on children's television.

But ... only six children from the class can attend. How will you decide who should go?

Activity

Read statements A–L. Decide which ones should be taken into account when making the decision about who should go. Put them in order of importance.

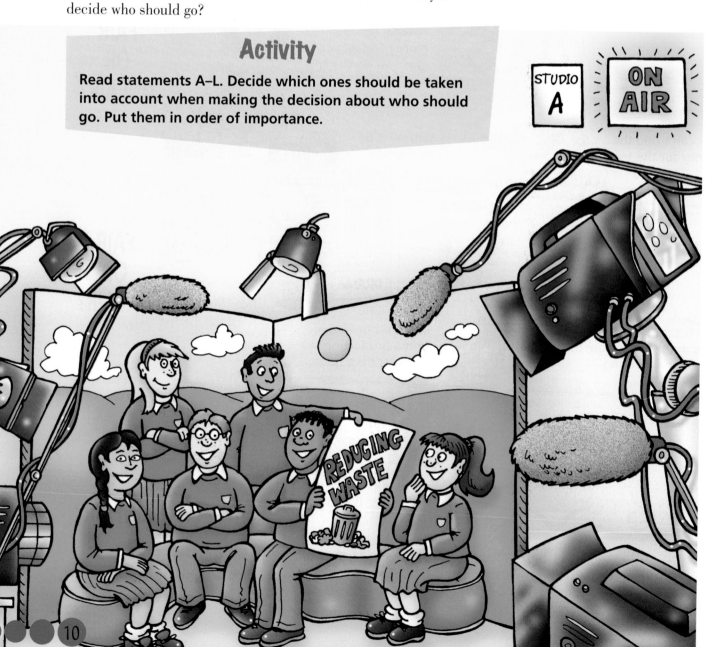

A Some pupils worked very hard, but did not produce much work that went into the class folder.

B Two pupils did a lot of the work at home using their parents' computers and colour printers.

C One pupil is very unhappy at the moment because of problems at home and it would really cheer her up.

D Several pupils do not have smart school uniforms.

E A group of pupils did a lot of work, but they have been misbehaving in some of their other lessons and are on report.

F Three pupils came to see you privately and begged to be allowed to go because they want to be on television.

G One pupil worked fairly hard on the project and missed a previous school treat because he was very ill. He is better now.

H A disagreement has been going on for some time between two pupils. An outing together might help them make up.

I The mother of one of the pupils was very interested in the competition and came in to class to help out.

J Two pupils have done a lot of excellent work, as usual. They have won prizes before because they are very clever.

K One pupil, who has produced some good work, suffers badly from asthma and might be ill if she gets too excited.

L It would be good to have equal numbers of boys and girls.

Discuss

1 a) How difficult did you find it to decide on the order of importance?
   b) Which of the statements should be taken into account? Why?
   c) Which ones should not be taken into account? Why?
   d) Are there any other ways in which the choice could be made? What are they?
2 a) Why is fairness so important to us?
   b) Why do we get so angry when we think we have been treated unfairly?
   c) Do you agree with people who say 'Tough! Life *is* unfair, you will just have to put up with it'?

People often think that it is unfair when their point of view is not listened to or taken into account. One way to make schools fairer is to involve pupils in making decisions about their school. Many schools have school councils to try to do this.

School councils are run differently in different schools. In most school councils, the pupils elect class representatives, who meet up regularly to discuss areas of interest and concern put forward by pupils in the school. The council's decisions are written down and put forward to the headteacher and governors of the school.

School councils have a number of purposes:

* to help everyone in the school to feel responsible for what goes on there
* to build everyone's confidence by giving them the chance to speak in public
* to give everyone the skills needed to work in groups
* to improve relationships between teachers and pupils
* to help pupils get on better with each other.

Activity

If you do not have a school council ...

1 Work in groups of four. Each group has to decide four things that would make a school council successful. Use these questions to help you:
   a) How should it be organised?
   b) How would people join?
   c) What sorts of topics should be discussed?
   d) What power should it have to change or influence what goes on in school?
   Remember that the teachers run the school and are responsible for discipline and safety. They have to have the final say.

2 Discuss your ideas as a class. Hold a series of votes until you come up with the sort of school council most of you can agree about.

3 Quite a lot of ideas about changing or improving our society are decided by voting. Not everybody's idea gets taken forward. What do you think about this way of making decisions?

Activity

If you already have a school council ...

1 Work in groups of four. Think about your school council:
   a) Read speech bubbles A–F and decide if you agree with any of them.
   b) What do you think about the way your school council is organised? Is it fair?
   c) Who represents your views?
   d) Does the council work well? Why or why not?
   e) What has your school council achieved?

2 a) In the same groups of four, decide three things that will improve the school council. These could be to do with:

   • how it is organised
   • the topics it discusses
   • what power it has to change or influence what goes on in the school.

   b) Discuss your ideas as a class. Each group calls out one idea at a time. This should be written on the board or a large sheet of paper. If an idea is put forward by more than one group, it should be ticked each time it is suggested.
   c) Pick the three ideas that have the most ticks and hold a vote on which improvement people think is the most important. You can then suggest this to your school council representative to mention at the next meeting.

3 What did you think about this process? Quite a lot of ideas for changing or improving our society are decided by voting and eliminating other possibilities. Not everybody's idea gets taken forward.

A It's always the same kinds of pupil who get elected – the clever ones.

B Whatever the school council decides, the headteacher will make the decisions. We can't really change things.

C Our school council helps us to have a real say in the things that affect us.

D I'm not interested in the school council. It's boring.

E We get on better with the teachers now that we have a school council. We understand their point of view.

F You get more confidence from being on the school council. It teaches you how to speak out.

Running a classroom council

Sometimes school councils do not work well. One reason might be that pupils have not learned how to make them work. Your class might find it useful to practise holding meetings and having debates.

Classroom constitution

You have to decide:

* what to discuss. You could set up a classroom council to discuss issues that affect you or as a way to hold debates.
* who will run the meetings. Probably the main posts you need to fill are a chairperson, a vice-chairperson and a secretary to keep notes.
* how to choose people for these posts
* how long people will stay in these posts (will they change every term, every half-term?)
* how often the class will meet as a council
* how the class will make decisions.

Make sure you write down the results of your decisions. This is your *constitution* for the classroom council.

Holding meetings

1 The first problem is to decide what to discuss. You need an agenda (items to discuss) for the meeting.
2 Then you need to elect a chairperson to run the meeting.

Look at the information on pages 15–16. It tells you how to write an agenda and how to run a meeting. It also suggests a way that you can elect a chairperson.

3 Now you need to decide on some topics for discussion. There are a few suggestions in the box on the right. Choose some of these and add some topics of your own.

Holding a debate

A debate is a much bigger discussion about one issue. There are rules for debates and you can read about these on page 16. Your class needs to choose a topic to debate. It could be:

'Experiments on animals are cruel. They should be stopped immediately.'

But you will probably want to choose your own topic. You might want to discuss a big issue that has just hit the news. Whatever you choose, the people arguing for the two sides of the debate should carry out some research so that they can develop a proper 'case' or argument for the position they support. It is no good just shouting your opinions at each other.

Topics for discussion

* How to deal with bullying in class
* Improving class rules
* Organising a class trip
* Brightening up the classroom
* Using the classroom at lunchtime
* Special events and fundraising

Elections

* You need to find out who would like to be considered for a post. Anyone interested should say so. This is called *standing* for the position. If more than one person would like to be considered, the class will need to vote.

* Each candidate should make a short speech about what they would do if elected to the post. Candidates might like to make election materials

Ballot Paper	
Vicky Garrett	
Cameron Hepburn	X
Davian Naipal	
Lisa Taylor	

(pamphlets or leaflets) to give out to the voters. In real elections, candidates have a team of people who support them and help with their campaign.

In all elections, the following rules apply:

* Everyone gets a vote, including the candidates standing for election.
* Votes are secret – you do not have to say who you have voted for if you don't want to.
* Voting is usually done by placing a cross (X) next to the person you have chosen on the paper (ballot paper).

BALLOT BOX

* Ballot papers are placed in a safe place, such as a sealed box, before the votes are counted.
* The time during which voting can take place is stated in advance and kept to.
* The candidates watch the votes being counted to make sure it is fair.

Agendas

* Before a classroom meeting, there should be an agenda that everyone can read. This has items for discussion at the meeting. The items are in the order they will be discussed. Meetings usually begin with apologies for absence and the minutes of the last meeting.

* There should be rules about how to get an item on to the agenda. You may decide that an item can only go on the agenda if two people or more put their names to the item. The class decides how long before the meeting the items should be given in: for example, no later than one day beforehand. If there are too many items for the meeting, some will have to be kept until a later meeting.

$$=\!\!= \text{AGENDA} =\!\!=$$
Items
1 Apologies for absence
2 Minutes of last meeting
3 Enlargement of school playing fields
4 Longer break times
5 Too much homework
6 Any other business

* You will also have to decide how long each item can have. One of the people suggesting the item will have to make a short speech about why the item is important.
* There should also be a short amount of time left at the end for *Any other business*. Only really short items are allowed here.

Running a meeting

* The chairperson is very important. They must make sure that:
  - the meeting gets through the items on the agenda
  - people who want to speak get a turn
  - people obey the rules of debating and do not interrupt each other
  - decisions are made on each item, if possible
  - everyone knows what will happen as a result of the decision.

* The chairperson must not take up time in the meeting giving their own opinions. Whether or not the chairperson agrees with someone else's opinions, that person must be allowed to speak. Anyone wishing to speak should raise a hand, but can speak only if the chairperson says so.

* At the beginning of each item, the chairperson should ask for a short introduction from the person who put the item on the agenda. When people have had their say about the item, depending on the time available, the chairperson should call for a vote. Usually, the vote has to be *for* or *against* something: for example, 'We propose that we should organise an event for Red Nose Day' – voting would be *yes* or *no*.

Debates

* You need a motion. Motions are worded in a particular way: for example, 'This house believes that bullies should be suspended from school every time they bully someone.'

* In the debate, a chairperson calls people to speak and makes sure they stick to the time given to them.

* Two people should speak 'for' the motion. Each speaker has a limited amount of time to make their case. The second speaker should add something new to the case, not just repeat what the first speaker has said.

* Two people should oppose the motion, again speaking in a limited time.

* Speakers can be interrupted during their speeches, but only in two ways:
  - If someone thinks the speaker is off the point, they can call 'point of order'. The chairperson asks the challenger to say what the point is and the chairperson decides whether or not it is a valid point.
  - if someone wants to ask a question or add some information, they can call 'point of information'. The speaker decides whether or not to allow this person to interrupt.

* When all speakers have finished, the debate is *opened to the floor* so that others can express their views. Anyone wanting to speak tries to catch the eye of the chairperson. The chairperson decides who should speak.

* After an agreed period of time, a vote is taken. You should vote for the motion, against the motion or abstain (not vote for either side). A count is taken and the motion is either *carried* or *defeated*.

section 2

Human rights and responsibilities – mutual respect and understanding
Whose rights? Whose responsibilities?

In a fair society, all people should expect to have basic rights and to be treated equally. Each of us is unique – everyone is different from everyone else. But differences should not be used to stop anyone getting fair treatment. The American Declaration of Independence (1776) says: 'We hold these truths to be self-evident, that all men are created equal, that they are endowed by their Creator with certain inalienable Rights, that among these are Life, Liberty and the pursuit of Happiness.'

Having rights does not mean that we can behave just as we like. Selfish or self-centred behaviour may infringe the rights of somebody else. We have to consider how our actions affect other people if our society is to be a pleasant place to live. We have responsibilities to our family and friends, our neighbours, people who live in our local community and the world outside. Rights and responsibilities are two sides of the same coin. You can't have one without the other.

In this section, you will learn about:

* types of intolerance
* differences in culture
* charters of human rights
* responsibilities.

You will:

* think about moral problems and decide what you think is right
* discuss these in small groups and in the whole class
* use your imagination to consider how other people might feel in different situations
* give your opinion and explain it to others.

Key words
- rights
- responsibility
- discrimination
- intolerance
- stereotype
- prejudice

Citizens of Planet Hoff

As a member of the United Council for Galactic Trade's team of investigators, you have already visited Planet Hoff in section 1 (see pages 2–3). This time the purpose of your team is to investigate the rights of Planet Hoff's citizens.

There are five main groups of citizens of Hoff. They are born into one of the groups. Very occasionally, a few citizens manage to move into higher groups.

Uppers rule Hoff. They are very rich and live in palaces or grand houses. They tell other citizens on the planet what to do. The Uppers are a very small group. The ruler of the planet – the Sesar of Hoff – is an Upper.

Capitos run the factories and workshops on Hoff that make goods. They sell these to the citizens of Hoff and trade them with other planets. Hoff is famous for its crystal clocks and hi-tech computer equipment. The Capitos also buy food cheaply from the farmer Doers (see opposite) and sell it in the cities for higher prices.

Some Capitos would like to move into the ranks of the Thinkers, who are seen as higher up in society. The high schools on Hoff are only open to the children of Thinkers. Every year a few Capito children are selected by exam to go to a high school. Other Capito children go to the low schools, which teach a limited number of subjects. Some Capitos would like to get jobs in the government, but they are rarely successful in job interviews.

Activity

1 **Identify what is unfair in Hoff society.**
2 **Recommend ways that Planet Hoff could change to improve the rights of all its citizens.**
3 **List at least five 'rights' that you think all citizens on Hoff should have.**

Thinkers help to run the planet, carrying out the orders of the Uppers. Most of the government is made up of Thinkers. Other Thinkers are doctors, lawyers and Knowers. Quite a lot of the Thinkers are involved in running the television stations on Hoff and writing electronic news sheets.

Some Thinkers want to have a say in how Hoff is run. They don't think that the Uppers should make all the decisions. When they organised meetings to protest, their leaders were arrested and the Uppers passed a law banning such meetings. The writers of electronic news sheets that criticised the Uppers were put in prison. The Uppers now insist on checking all news sheets before they are sent out.

Doers work in factories or on farms. Their wages are fixed at a low level by the Uppers and they all have to work long hours every week. However, they are guaranteed a home to live in and the price of basic foods is fixed. Medical treatment is free and excellent. The Uppers want to keep the Doers fit and healthy so that they can work.

The Doers are not allowed to move to other parts of Hoff unless they get government permission. They need special passes, and if the police find them without a pass, they are imprisoned. The Doers are not allowed to go to government schools. They are selected to do a certain job and shown how to do it. They run their own free schools for a few hours every day in buildings where they can find some space. Many Doers have shown themselves to be very clever, but young Doers start work very young, so they don't have much time for education.

Gronks are at the bottom of society. They are not free. They are owned by Uppers or Thinkers, and do all the domestic jobs like cooking and cleaning in the homes of their owners. They have electronic implants in their heads which allow their owners to control them. If they have children, the children become the property of the owner; they have an implant put in their heads when they are five years old. The Gronks can be bought and sold. They have their own religion, but they are not allowed to worship their gods. They are severely beaten if caught doing so.

CITIZEN ZONE

HOFF CITY

You can find out more about Planet Hoff on pages 2–3, 62–63 and 90–91.

2.2 What is a stereotype and why does it matter?

We often think we know what someone is like, even though we have never met that person. We base our opinions on stereotypes.

Stereotypes are descriptions of groups of people who have something in common, such as their age, their religion, their sex or their nationality. The description is applied to everyone in the group and ignores the individual differences between people.

So people might say:

* 'If they are old/young, they must be …'
* 'If they are Christian/Muslim, they must be …'
* 'If they're boys/girls, they must be …'
* 'If they are from country X, they must be …'

People often do have something in common with others of the same sex, age, race or religion, but it does not mean that they all think or act in the same way.

1 Work in pairs. On a large sheet of paper, draw a stereotype of a young person today. Label the picture to show the kind of clothes that they would wear. Also show by labels or drawings this person's interests, tastes in music, etc.

2 Display the pictures around the room. Compare them. Put them into groups.

3 a) Do your pictures give an accurate image of young people today?
   b) Are all young people like the ones in the pictures?
   c) Where do stereotypes of young people come from?

A housewife

You Englanders have won this time but I vill have my revenge!

A German soldier in the Second World War

4 Working in groups of four or five, look at the five pictures on these two pages.
   a) Decide what each picture is suggesting about the people shown.
   b) Do you think all the people in the group shown are like this?
   c) How do illustrations like this make us think about certain groups of people?
   d) Why do people use stereotypes like these in comics, cartoons and magazines?

A granny

Hunters

A football supporter

5 a) What other stereotypes have you heard about?
b) Where have you heard or seen them?
c) Where do you think stereotypes come from?
d) Why do people believe them?
e) How do they affect the way people treat each other?
f) How might they affect the way you see yourself and what you do in the future?

Challenging stereotypes

Have you heard this story? A little boy was knocked down on his way to school. He was walking along, holding his father's hand, when a lorry hit him. He was rushed to hospital in an ambulance and taken straight to the operating theatre. The surgeon came in, gasped and exclaimed, 'That's my son!' What is the relationship of the surgeon to the boy?
*See the note below for the answer.

6 Write out the situations A–E and complete them in a way that challenges stereotypes, using one of phrases 1–5 from the list below.

A *Two lorry drivers were sitting in a transport café chatting about their difficult journey. On the way back to their lorries, one of the lorry drivers ...*

B *A motor-bike rider was stopped by the police for speeding. The police officer noted his age, and said ...*

C *The athlete who won the marathon was very fit. She also had the very latest...*

D *The teacher amused his pupils by telling stories of his holidays. His most recent holiday was ...*

E *The football team was ecstatic to win. They rushed back to the changing rooms to get ready for their night out ...*

1 ... to visit his family in India.

2 ... lightweight wheelchair

3 ... called her husband on her mobile phone.

4 ... at a hen party.

5 ... at 65 you should know better.

7 Working in pairs, make up three more examples of your own, like the ones above.

*The surgeon was the boy's mother. This story challenges a stereotype of the kinds of work that women do.

2.3 How can you challenge racism?

Some of the most damaging stereotypes are racial stereotypes. We attach certain characteristics to people from a particular ethnic group or who come from a particular country. We all know about the image of Germans and the Second World War. We know that some people in European countries think that all young Englishmen are football hooligans, yobs and lager louts.

These stereotypes are based on prejudice – opinions that people form without knowing all the facts. People often make up their minds quickly about other people without knowing much about them or taking the time to get to know them. Prejudices can be harmful when people are treated unfairly because of them. When people are treated unfairly because of prejudice about their race or colour, they are the victims of racial discrimination and this is against the law.

Prejudice can lead to people calling others racist names, taunting them about the colour of their skin and making their lives uncomfortable. In the worst cases, it can lead to actual violent attacks. Read the following case studies.

Case study 1: Maqsood Ahmad

Maqsood Ahmad talks about his experiences of racism in Rochdale...

"My earliest memories of racism are from a school in Rochdale, where I grew up; I remember people not sitting next to me, throwing things and calling me names. There were only two or three Asians in my class. Young people then just accepted it; got on as best they could. The teachers saw it as children playing pranks. Then you started missing lessons because you were frightened to go into the classroom, so you'd get into trouble with the teachers. It was a hostile environment for people like me. Even outside the school you couldn't really get away from it. My mother wouldn't let me play football outside; she wanted to protect me, but you end up excluded [cut off] from society.

[When I was older] I realised I couldn't get away from racism. You get your windows smashed, dog dirt through your letter box, your mother is spat at when she goes to the shops, your sister is sworn at and her headscarf is pulled off. It all made me very angry. Only the good sense of my mother and father made me see that not every white person is racist. That's why I got into working against racism.

If you are attacked on a regular basis, you get worn down. Every time you meet someone you wonder, "Are they treating me differently?" Even if they are not, you are suspicious because of your experience. If my parents hadn't kept talking to me about these issues, I think I'd have ended up hating white people; it's a common reaction.

Racist organisations were very active in Rochdale when I was growing up. These organisations always breed in areas where they can get support. If no action is taken, it becomes a confident environment for them. But in areas where communities are strong, with good anti-racist activists and a good strong police force that will take strong action and root these individuals out, others don't express these views."

Activity

Sometimes we see racism going on around us, but don't know what we can do to help prevent it. Look at the following chart in which some suggestions have been made. Discuss these suggestions in small groups and try to think of other ways in which people could have helped Maqsood.

Maqsood's experiences	What could have been done to help
People wouldn't sit next to him at school	Class sit alphabetically. Discussions in class about why people from the Commonwealth were invited to come to UK.
Things thrown at him. Maqsood called names. Teachers saw it as children playing pranks	School policy on bullying. Class discussion on bullying. Maqsood gets support from his peers (people of around the same age).
Mother protected Maqsood and he felt excluded	Friends call round at his house and meet his family. They invite him to play football with them.
Racist organisations	Classmates and friends find out the facts about racist political parties and the law that aims to protect minority ethnic groups (see pages 37–38).

Case study 2: Samantha Corbin

Samantha Corbin, a young black woman, talks about her experiences of racism when she was younger...

"My earliest memories of racism come from when I was growing up in East London. I remember the older boys who lived on the estate weren't a nice bunch. When I used to play outside they would taunt me by calling me racist names. When I started at my infant/junior school I remember that I was the only black girl, although there were more children from the Asian community. This made me nervous.

When I entered secondary school I was hoping that things would change, the name calling, but it actually got worse. Boys and girls made comments and passed notes about me to make me feel uncomfortable. The boys encouraged the girls to be unpleasant. The girls would find ways to exclude me from their groups. Say, for instance, they were talking about make-up, they would say "You can't wear this because your skin is too dark."

I remember clearly a girl made a comment as I sat on the chair next to her: "Oh, I'm not allowed to sit next to you as my dad doesn't like spades." This really angered me as I had not done anything except sit at the desk next to her. So I got up and shouted at her. This started a big fight. We got separated and sent to the Head of Year. From that day she never bothered me again with her comments. Mum would say, "Try not to get yourself involved in a fight but you must be proud of who you are and what you are! These children have not been properly educated to respect other people's individuality, creed and colour." My mum wanted her children to get the most out of *(continued on the next page)* their education so they could get better jobs in the future.

Something I realise was that I was always into sport. I was sometimes removed from my lessons to represent the school in netball, basketball, rounders and athletics. This was not a problem when it came to trophies and medals for the school. When I was successful, children became nice and polite, including the child who was verbally abusive towards me.

Outside school I used to attend a local youth club. One evening my friend and I were coming home and we heard some loud voices behind us talking in a racist way. When they emerged from behind the streetlights, we saw six tall guys with bald heads coming towards us. The only thing we could do was to run for our lives. I was very scared. My mother told us about her experiences of racism and said it was better to get out of difficult situations like that.

Activity

1 Work in pairs again. See if you can suggest some things that could have been done to help prevent the racism that Samantha experienced.

Samantha's experiences	What could have been done to help

2 a) What different ideas have people suggested for helping to prevent racism?

   b) Compare the two ways in which Maqsood and Samantha dealt with racism.

3 Sometimes people are racist in our presence. It is important, but difficult, to challenge these people.

   Working in pairs, write down how you would deal with the following situations:

   a) A member of your family makes a racist comment while you are watching a television programme.

   b) A friend points to someone in the street and calls out a racist name.

   c) A member of your class refuses to work in your group with someone because of their race or ethnic group.

   d) Two older boys are bullying a younger Muslim boy, pushing him around and making jokes about his mother's headscarf.

   e) Someone at your youth club tells you a racist joke.

4 Discuss in class what different pairs have suggested for the above situations, and the problems involved in taking a stand.

Kick it out!

Challenging racism can be difficult, but it *can* be done and things *can* change. For many years, particularly in the 1970s and 1980s, black football players suffered abuse and racist chants at football matches. People from ethnic minorities did not go to football matches for fear that they would be harassed and intimidated.

In the early 1990s, a campaign called 'Let's Kick Racism Out of Football' was launched by football clubs and supporters' groups along with organisations like the Commission for Racial Equality. Clubs agreed to a plan to challenge racism inside football stadiums. They put anti-racist statements in programmes, on posters and around the grounds. Lots of clubs worked on their own anti-racist schemes with youth groups and schools in their local area. The campaign also encouraged players to speak out about the racism they faced.

Artwork from a resource pack produced by *Show Racism the Red Card*, an organisation formed by the Professional Footballers Association, the European Union and UNISON to fight racism in all its forms.

1 To issue a statement saying the club will not tolerate racism, spelling out the action it will take against those engaged in racist chanting. The statement should be printed in all match programmes and displayed permanently and prominently around the ground.

2 Make public address announcements condemning racist chanting at matches.

3 Make it a condition for season ticket holders that they do not take part in racial abuse.

4 Take action to prevent the sale of racist literature inside and around the ground.

5 Take disciplinary action against players who engage in racial abuse.

An extract from the ten-point plan produced by clubs

The campaign has been very successful. Most black players say that the situation now is much better than it was ten years ago. There has been a real attempt to develop a feeling in football grounds that racism is not acceptable. But the problems have not disappeared. Some players still face racist abuse from fans and many families from minority ethnic groups do not feel confident about attending football matches. Also few Asian players are coming through into professional football, despite the fact that football is extremely popular among Asians in Britain today.

The campaign against racism in football is carried on by Kick It Out, an organisation specially set up by football associations. Kick It Out works with professional clubs and groups in amateur football to raise awareness of and wipe out racism in football, whether played in a stadium or in a park.

An illustration from the *Show Racism the Red Card* resource pack.

Some extracts from an interview with Andy Cole talking about his experiences of racism in football:

Is there any one incident (of racism) in football that sticks in your mind?

When I was a teenager looking to join a club I was at one ground and a certain player came up to me and goes, 'Are you all right Chalkie?' which just set my mind against that club there and then, and I just decided that I wouldn't be signing for them. To be honest, it would have been better for me personally if I signed for that club at that time, but that incident changed my mind and I went to Arsenal instead. I never had any trouble at Arsenal. There were a lot of black pros in the team at the time – Paul Davis, Michael Thomas, David Rocastle – people like that – so it was better for me.

Extracts from an interview by Nick Varley, published in *Kick It Out* in conjunction with *Shoot*.

What happened with your family?

They came up to a game (at Newcastle) one day and suffered quite a bit of racist abuse outside the ground. I was really disappointed for my family to experience that because I'd been there for so long without any problems. I thought it was bang out of order. They were coming up to support me, like a lot of other fans, and they got that.

And what about in the stands?

Well, some people don't want to speak out because they don't want to get involved, but those who do will be the ones who get things moving. Then other people sitting next to them will say, 'I don't want to hear that sort of thing', and they can get them ejected.

That's where it's going to stop. Only when people themselves make a stand and say, 'I'm not having that'. Sometime you will have to stand up against your brother, sister, mum or dad and show them your beliefs. At the end of the day it doesn't matter how racist you are, you will know in yourself that it's wrong to hate someone because of the colour of their skin.

Here is what Manchester United hero Ryan Giggs, whose father is black, has to say about his experiences:

'You come across the odd bit of racism both in primary and secondary school. It's similar to bullying. I mean, as a kid it affects your whole life, so it's not very nice when it's happening to you. Talk to someone. Teachers, maybe parents, can help you because, as I say, you can't let it affect your school work, affect your life and make it a misery.'

GIRLS' AND WOMEN'S FOOTBALL

Football is an increasing passion for young Asian women. More and more are taking up the game and enjoying the opportunities available to play from grassroots up to international level…
In fact women's football is the fastest growing sport in this country.

Permi Jahooti plays right wing-back for Chelsea ladies after spells with Fulham and Millwall. At 28 Permi is an accomplished player who is set to play for the Indian national team.

Activity

1 Racism does not just occur in football. It can occur in other areas of sport for men and women. What can you do to prevent racism in sport:
   a) in your own teams (e.g. picking teams, training, in the changing rooms)
   b) when other teams come to play against you (e.g. how you welcome them, things you say to them on the playing field)
   c) as a supporter of your local team (e.g. on the touchline, things you cheer and shout)
   d) as a fan of a national team (e.g. talking about new players, things you say about other teams)?
2 You could design, paint or draw your own anti-racist statements. These could be paintings like the ones on pages 25 and 26. But you could also design posters, postcards, T-shirts or badges. Think carefully about the message you want to put on your design. Will it be a single powerful image or will you have some suggestions for ways of combating racism?

Note: You can find some advice on what you can do if you are a victim of racial abuse and bullying on Info page 38.

2.4 What rights should all children have?

Do you feel that you have sometimes been treated unfairly by adults? Most young people do not usually have much trouble in answering this question.

Children often feel that adults stop them from doing things they have a right to do. Adults, for their part, justify their actions by saying that they are protecting the child or looking after the child's interests. Some adults think that children do not have rights at all and that they are not able to decide matters for themselves.

Activity

1 Think of two or three occasions when an adult stopped you doing something that you feel you had a right to do. Discuss them in class.

2 What rights should all children have? Read the speech bubbles on these pages with a partner. Note down the rights that you think are really important. Note the ones you do not think are important or can't decide about. You could write them in a table like the one below. The first one has been done for you.

It is important that children should have the right to . . .	It is not very important that children should have the right to . . .	Children should NOT have the right to . . .
free education		

A I should have the right to free education.

B I should have the right to go to bed when I want to.

C I should be able to get enough food to keep me healthy.

D I should have the right to stay with my family or the people who love me and want to look after me.

E I should have the right to drink alcohol.

F There should be times when I can play and relax.

G I should be able to go out and stay out until I decide it's time to come home.

H I should have the right to work to earn money to help my family.

I Adults should not bully me, beat me or abuse me in any way.

J Adults should listen to my views when they make a decision that will affect my life.

K I should have the right to eat sweets when I want to.

L I should have the right to decide what I learn at school.

M I should have the right to special care and education if I am disabled.

N I should have the right to watch whatever I like on television.

O I should be allowed to develop my abilities and talents to the fullest.

P I should have the right to use a credit card.

Discuss

Discuss these questions as a whole class:
a) **Which rights were you not sure about and why?**
b) **Which did you think were really important rights?**
c) **Which were not so important?**
d) **Which were not really important at all?**
e) **Which other rights would you add to the ones you have said were important?**

Convention on the Rights of the Child

The United Nations has drawn up a list of rights that all children should have.

Some of the main points from this list are shown in the scroll on the right. The idea behind many of these rights is that children should be protected and given the chance to develop their abilities as useful members of society. It is not legally binding and in many countries it is completely ignored.

Discuss

Did your list of important rights on page 28 match the United Nations Convention?

Setting out the rights that children should have is one thing. Making sure that they get their rights is something else. In the case studies below you will see examples of different ways in which children's rights are abused.

United Nations Convention on the Rights of the Child

Children should have the right to:

- free education
- enough food to eat and clean water to drink
- medical care to help them stay healthy
- play and time for leisure
- not suffer from discrimination
- live with their family or those who love them best
- be protected from physical, mental and sexual abuse
- have special care if they are disabled
- a name and nationality
- know what their rights are
- enjoy these rights whatever their colour, religion or gender, whether they are rich or poor, and whether or not they are disabled

Case study 1: Street child in Africa

Kwame was fourteen years old. He lived in a village about 170 km north of Accra, the capital of Ghana. His father worked on a cocoa farm, but his work was not regular and he could not pay Kwame's school fees. In Ghana, you can't go to school if you can't pay. Knowing he was about to be forced to leave school, Kwame decided he had to seek a better life elsewhere. He borrowed some money from his friends, walked 13 km to a larger village with a lorry station and hitched a ride to Accra. He arrived on a Thursday night – alone, tired and very confused. That night he slept in the lorry park.

He soon discovered that life on the streets was tough. In the first week he was beaten up by other boys, City Guards and the police. He was lucky to find other boys from his district with whom he could stay. He slept in an open courtyard with about 200 other boys. It was not much of a place, but it was somewhere to sleep in relative safety.

After ten days, Kwame got his first job as a rubbish carrier in the markets. He worked three times a day – at 3 a.m., 11 a.m. and 6 p.m. – but at least he had enough work to scrape a living. He began to get streetwise. He learned to hit first and talk later. He discovered how important it was to

Read the case studies on pages 30–32 and decide which of the rights set out in the United Nations Convention are being denied to the children described.

Case study 2: Child miners in Bolivia

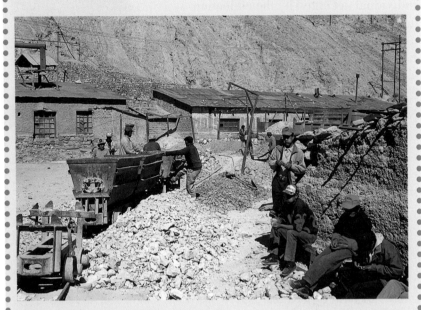

be part of a gang who offered some protection. He tried marijuana and found hard liquor.

Two years later, Kwame is a shoe shine boy. His day starts at sunrise when he buys water to wash and pays for the privilege of using a pit latrine. If he has enough money left from the day before he will buy something to eat and water to drink. Then his working day begins as he moves around the city looking for customers. At the end of a good day he might have made as much as £1.50, which will go towards his food. At the end of a bad day he will go hungry. Each night he returns to the same spot, in the same courtyard, to sleep. As none of the boys' possessions are safe here, he pays one of the boys to act as a night watchman to look after his shoe shine box. It is his most prized possession, the symbol of his status in street society, and as such he will guard it fiercely and fight violently to defend it.

Source: Case study supplied by Street Child Africa

Elias and Ramiro Jankho are brothers who work in the Santa Rosa mine, digging for silver, lead and zinc. Ramiro, who is twelve years old, pushes a wheelbarrow of rough metal ore through the dark passageways of the mine. His ten-year-old brother, Elias, helps him heave it up to the surface in a bucket attached to a rope.

The mine is a lightless cave, reached by a narrow passage through the rock. You have to bend double in places to get through. At one point the brothers lower themselves down through a hole in the rock floor to a ledge and from there climb down a rickety wooden ladder – all this by the lamp glowing dimly on another miner's helmet. The boys do not have helmets and there is no safety system in the mine. Miners hack ore from the rock with hammer and chisel much as they did 400 years ago. Many of them become ill from the dust and grit in the mine.

The boys are not paid for their work. They are there to help their father earn a living – around £2.70 per day for an adult miner. Sometimes they get food and clothes. They don't work in the mine all the time. Both go to school but not regularly. Ramiro has worked in the mine since he was eight. 'Now I come every day, except when there's school,' he said. 'Then I study in the morning and come to the mine in the afternoon. I help my brother get out the ore.' Elias works in the mine less often. 'I help my father. I shovel ore. I get tired sometimes but I rest inside the mine.'

Source: Case study written by Chris Holt for Cafod

Our last case study is different. It is about someone who struggled to get her rights as an individual accepted by the education authorities.

Case study 3: Katie Caryer

I am sixteen and have cerebral palsy. Cerebral palsy is a general term for physical disability caused by damage to the brain. No two people with CP are the same; like no two people with black hair are the same. In my case, my limbs and mouth haven't a good contact system to my brain. I can't talk with my mouth and I am really wobbly. I use an electronic communication aid and a wheelchair for long walks. In every other respect, I am a typical teenager.

I go to a local school because I am a local kid. However, I had a big struggle to get in. In education law, disabled kids don't have the right to go to their local school like everyone else. Councils can force disabled children into segregated special schools miles away from their local community against their or their family's wishes. My mum ended up having to go to the High Court. Some of my disabled mates' families have moved miles away to get what we call inclusive education, i.e. going to your local school and being welcome there. Being at your local school isn't the end of the story. I couldn't use the lift for a whole year because the school said it was dangerous because it was a goods lift. Having to struggle up three flights of stairs with my wobbly legs and poor balance was probably much more dangerous. The school made the mistake of thinking that everyone has to be treated the same, even if it means denying someone equal opportunities.

My head of year told my best friend not to spend time with me and to find other friends "because you'll never be able to do things like go to the cinema with Katie". Weird idea – this summer with my friends I've been flying in a microlight plane, been on the London Eye and been to see the Rocky Horror Show in fishnet stockings and suspenders.

Still, my education experience is better than if I was placed in a segregated school. I am pushed to do well and most of my mates I've met through school. Segregated kids don't bother with education for one reason or another.

Working children

Should children have the right to work? In some examples, like case study 2 on page 31, it is clear that working very long hours affects children's health, their chances of obtaining an education and their ability to have some play and leisure time to themselves. Yet many children in countries where there is child labour often say that they want to be able to work because they want to earn money to help their families. But they also want to:

* work shorter hours
* receive fair pay
* have time to themselves to play
* be able to go to school.

What about the UK?

In the UK, children have to go to school. They are not allowed to work until they are thirteen years old and then they are only allowed to work a certain number of hours a week. However, it is estimated that over 600,000 children are working illegally in the UK, mainly because they are under age. What are your attitudes towards young people working?

Discuss

1 **What difficulties did Katie have to overcome?**
2 **What problems does she still have to face?**
3 **What rights does Katie feel are being denied to many disabled children?**
4 **What happens/might happen to disabled pupils in your school?**
5 **How easy is it/would it be for them to take a full part in school life?**

Activity

Look at scenarios A–F on this page. All of the young people are over 13 years old and legally able to work. In each case decide:

a) whether the work is having, or might have, a damaging effect on their education

b) whether they should work or not.

A Michael helps out in his family newsagent's shop before he goes to school. He has to get up at 6a.m. to receive the newspapers and write the delivery addresses on them, ready for the newspaper deliverers. He also serves behind the counter when he gets home. His teachers have noticed that he is very tired at school.

B Stephen lives at home with his mother, who is a single parent. He knows that they are short of money and he now feels that he is old enough to help out. He wants to deliver newspapers. But his mother does not want him to go out on dark mornings and she is worried that it will affect him at school. She says he can't do it.

C Jo wants a mobile phone and more clothes. Her parents say it will cost too much and that if she wants all these things, she will have to get a part-time job. She says that the parents of her friends pay for their phones and clothes, and she does not see why she has to work.

D Sita wants to earn some money to buy Christmas presents for her family and friends. Her father has refused to let her work. He says that he will give her the money.

E John works on a street market one day a week. He really enjoys working with his uncle on his fruit and vegetable stall. The problem is that market day is also a day when he should be at school. The Education Welfare Officer says that he will take the family to court if John does not attend school.

F Parul gets pocket money but does not do a lot around the house. However, she is desperate to go on a school trip with her friends. Her parents say that they will pay half if she pays half. She will have to work to get the money.

Discuss

Discuss the following issues as a whole class:

a) whether children should work at all

b) at what age and for how long

c) what other limits you would set.

In the park

dog owner

children

park keeper

mother and toddler

At the shopping centre

shopkeepers

shoppers

shoplifters

shopping centre manager

security guards

On the road

motor cyclist

pedestrians

cyclist

car drivers

Activity

1 Work in groups of three or four. Choose one of the scenes to think about. Different groups in the class should choose different scenes. Then discuss the following questions:
   a) What responsibilities do the named people in your scene have in that situation or place?
   b) Why are these responsibilities important?
   c) What would be irresponsible behaviour by each of them?
   d) What could happen if they behaved irresponsibly?

2 Write up your answers and pin them on the notice board around an enlarged photocopy of the picture. One member of your group should explain to the rest of the class what you have written.

headteacher

parents

teacher

pupils

DANGEROUS FENCE

At school

A question of responsibilities

Sometimes it is not easy to decide where our responsibilities lie.
We are pulled in different directions.

1 Working in threes, role play the following situations. In each one, the person playing the pupil should first act out a scene with the person playing the teacher and then act out a scene with the third person. At the end of each situation, try to agree on how you could resolve the conflicting responsibilities.

2 Some groups could role play each situation to the class so that everyone can discuss the issues raised.

3 Discuss any situation where you think young people are pulled in different directions and the sorts of problems this creates for people trying to act responsibly.

Situation 1

Pupil	Teacher	Friend
You are very proud to be a member of the school swimming team. The PE teacher has said that every member of the team must attend training sessions every week.	You expect everyone to attend training sessions to stay in the team. It is the main rule of membership. If anyone misses training, they will lose a place in the team.	You are having a special event for your birthday and want your best friend to come, but it is on the same evening as training for the swimming team. Your friend is in the team.

Situation 2

Pupil	Teacher	Grandparent
You are late with a piece of coursework for Geography. You have been given one more chance to complete the work. If you don't get it in tomorrow, you will get a low grade and be kept in detention.	Some of the pupils in your class have been very slow to complete homework and have been warned already. Tomorrow is their last chance to get it in. Detentions will be given to anyone who fails to hand in the coursework.	You are worried about a form that you should have filled in for the council to apply for a home help. You need someone to help you complete it, so you ask your grandchild to come over for the evening.

Situation 3

Pupil	Teacher	Parent
The drama teacher has asked to see you. You hope the teacher is going to ask you to be involved in the school show. However, your mother has said that you must baby-sit this evening while she goes out.	The school show is due to open tomorrow and the scenery is still not painted. One of your pupils is very good at painting and keen to be involved in the show. You ask if the pupil will help out this evening for a little while.	You have been invited out with a friend in the early evening – you haven't been out for a long time. You have insisted that your child looks after the baby, otherwise they will get no pocket money this month.

2.6 Prejudice, discrimination and racism

Prejudice and discrimination

* Prejudices are opinions that we form without knowing all the facts or much information. They are attitudes.
* Discrimination means treating someone unfairly because of your prejudice. It involves actions.

Many of the prejudices we have are harmless. But prejudices are harmful if they mean that people are treated unfairly because of them. Treating someone unfairly because of prejudices about their race or colour is called racial discrimination. Racial discrimination is against the law.

The law about race

* In the United Kingdom, the Race Relations Act of 1976 makes it against the law to discriminate against anyone because of their race, colour, nationality or ethnic origin. This applies to jobs, training, housing, education and the provision of goods and services.
* Racial violence is an offence under the criminal law. Inciting or encouraging racial hatred is also an offence under the criminal law. This means that if you are found guilty, you become a criminal and can be sent to prison.
* Racial prejudice is not against the law because an attitude cannot be made illegal.

What are Racial Equality Councils?

* The Commission for Racial Equality was set up in 1976 to tackle issues of racial discrimination across the UK, to work for racial equality and to encourage good relations between people from different racial backgrounds. It receives government money.
* There are just over a hundred Racial Equality Councils in the UK, which tackle racial discrimination and try to encourage good relations in local communities.

Some background history

For centuries, people have come to the UK from many parts of the world, for all sorts of reasons:

* The Romans, Anglo-Saxons and Normans came as invaders.
* Others came to trade or work here.
* Many came to escape war, famine or religious hatred, such as the Huguenots and Jewish and Irish people.
* People from countries such as India, Bangladesh, Pakistan and the West Indies were invited here after the Second World War to fill job vacancies.

Remember that the UK built up a huge empire during the eighteenth and nineteenth centuries. It ruled large parts of the world – in India, Africa, China, the West Indies and many other places – as colonies. Lots of British people went to live in the colonies and control large areas of territory. The UK has a special relationship with the people who come from the former colonies. Many thousands fought for the UK in the two world wars of the twentieth century. For instance, over 1 million Indians died fighting for the British in the First World War.

After the Second World War, when British colonies became independent, many of them decided that they did not want to lose all their links with the UK. So they joined the Commonwealth, which is a voluntary organisation of 54 former British colonies. They co-operate to promote the common interests of their peoples.

The UK has always been a place where people with roots in other parts of the world have lived. In 1764, for instance, there were about 20,000 black people living in London. There have always been different communities in which not everyone was the same. Today, well over 3 million people in the UK call themselves 'black', 'Asian' or 'Chinese', or say they belong to another group. Nearly half were born and brought up in the UK, which is now their country of origin.

Source: Much of the above material was adapted from the CRE pamphlet 'No Room for Racism'.

What can you do if you are the victim of racist abuse and bullying?

* You don't have to accept it. We all have a right to live without this sort of hassle.

* Realise it's not your problem. It's hard to walk away from bullies, but it's not your fault and you haven't done anything to make people torment you in this way.

* Tell someone what's happening to you. Try talking to a teacher or a parent if you can. Telling someone is the first step in sorting the problem out. Find someone you can trust before the problem spirals out of control.

* If a group of you is being targeted, raise the issue at school in discussion lessons and tutorials, or at the school council.

* Keep a note of what is happening. This might be useful to show others what is happening to you.

* Don't rise to the problem. There is little point in arguing back to racists. It will only incite them to make the taunts worse and more often. Instead, try to seek help and talk about it.

* Be aware. You can't spend your life worrying about racists, but do be careful not to take unnecessary risks. Try not to walk about on your own in areas where you know people who taunt you will be.

* Stay confident. Don't let racists ruin your life. This isn't easy, but it is important to make sure you keep your self-esteem.

* Don't give up. It may well stop if you don't let it bother you. Keep talking about it and try not to let it get you down!

Source: Adapted from an article by Tamara Wilder of Victim Support in the *Show Racism the Red Card* resource book.

Local government and community
Who's running the area you live in?

Most of us live in a community that gives us a sense of belonging. People have different ideas about what a community is. For some people it is about their neighbours and the jobs people do, such as farming or fishing; for others it is to do with their religious beliefs. Sometimes people develop their sense of belonging by facing a common challenge, like pulling together in the face of floods or being a minority in a larger community. Many of us are part of several communities that overlap – for example, our family, friends and neighbours, our school and the ethnic group to which we belong.

Often when we use the word 'community' we mean the people who live near us and around us in a particular area. What happens in our area usually has a big effect on our lives. So we need to look at who makes the decisions about the things that influence our daily lives and who runs the basic services on which we depend.

In this section you will learn about:

* how local government works
* who makes decisions about local matters
* voting in local elections
* planning and the impact of developments on different groups in the community
* services and amenities in your local community
* voluntary organisations in your community.

You will:

* present your ideas
* think about issues and decide what you would do
* support a case you may not believe in
* use your imagination to consider how other people might feel in different situations
* express your opinion and explain it to others.

Key words
* community
* councillor
* election
* policy
* services

What do you do if nobody is emptying your dustbins?

What do you do if your neighbours are really noisy and keep you awake?

How can you make the streets look better in the area around your home and where you go to school?

The answer to all these questions is – **contact your local council!** Councils are responsible for many of the services in your local area. Everybody wants to live in clean streets, to have their rubbish collected regularly, and to walk and play in well-kept parks. These services make a big difference to the quality of people's everyday lives. Not all councils provide the same services, but they tend to cover the areas shown in the illustration on pages 42–43.

Activity

Work in pairs or threes. The people below have all come to the council for advice and help. But they don't know where to go. Can you help them?

For each of the six cases shown here:
a) decide which department the people could go to for help
b) suggest what you think this council department can do, if anything, to help
c) decide what you think would be the best solution to the situation. (This may not only be what the council can do but also what other people can do.)

Use the illustration of the council on pages 42–43 to find your answers.

1 **Hilda Bakewell and her family have had just about enough of their next-door neighbours, the Wilkinsons. During the daytime and into the evening, the Wilkinson children play their music so loud that the Bakewells can hardly hear the television. They come in late at night, sometimes at 2 or 3a.m., and always wake up the Bakewells with their laughter, shouting and swearing.**

2 Mrs K. Blink is 85 years old and lives on her pension. She has no other money. She lives on her own in a block of flats. But her neighbours never go to see her to find out if she is all right. She cannot walk very far. She cannot do her shopping and needs someone to help her clean her flat.

3 John Costa's house has been repossessed because he was made redundant and could not pay the mortgage payments. He has a wife, an aunt and three children living with him. They desperately need accommodation.

4 Bob and Martha Jenkins cannot pay their council tax bills. They are both over 50 years old and are unable to get work. They get unemployment benefit, but they cannot save enough money to pay the huge council tax bill in one go. If they do not pay their bill, they can be taken to court.

5 Betty and Winston Smith and several other residents are very concerned about a new office block, which is being built behind their house. They were consulted about the original plans, but the block seems to be much higher than the plans showed. They are sure it is going to make their houses dark and stop them getting sunlight in their gardens. They are also concerned about the noise, dust and dirt coming off the site on to their houses.

6 Marian Abbot has just arrived in the area with her two children. She wants to find out about the schools that her children can go to in the area and what she has to do to get them in. In their previous school, the children were identified as 'gifted children' with special abilities in maths and sciences. Marian wants them to get the right schooling to help them develop their talents.

Discuss

1 When you have worked through all the cases, present your answers to the rest of the class and see if you agree, particularly about the best ways of dealing with the problems.

2 Have a class discussion about whether or not the people in a community should leave it to the council to deal with these and other local problems, such as noisy neighbours, keeping the local area tidy, local schools. What part, if any, should local people play?

You have probably heard about councillors. These are people who are elected to run the council. We will look at them more closely later on in this section. But there are also council officers. They do the day-to-day business of running the council. They organise and run the services that the council provides. Lots of people work for the council doing various jobs, such as giving information to the public and handling complaints.

Finance

This department deals with:
- council tax bills and enquiries
- housing benefits
- council rents.

Environmental services

This department is responsible for:
- street cleaning and rubbish collection
- environmental health, including food safety and pest control
- air quality, noise pollution and noise patrol
- giving licences to pubs, clubs and events
- trading standards – making sure shops are selling safe products and not cheating people
- improving the area – making changes to streets and buildings.

Leisure and amenities

This department looks after:
- parks and open spaces
- recycling centres
- recreation and sports centres
- libraries
- cemeteries
- youth clubs and schemes for young people.

Planning and technical services

This department is responsible for:
- giving permission for new buildings – houses, flats, offices and other business premises
- housing improvement – when people want to add extra rooms to, or change certain features of, their houses
- highways, pavements and engineering works – digging up roads for pipes, putting in road humps, etc.
- crime prevention, including closed-circuit television (CCTV) cameras.

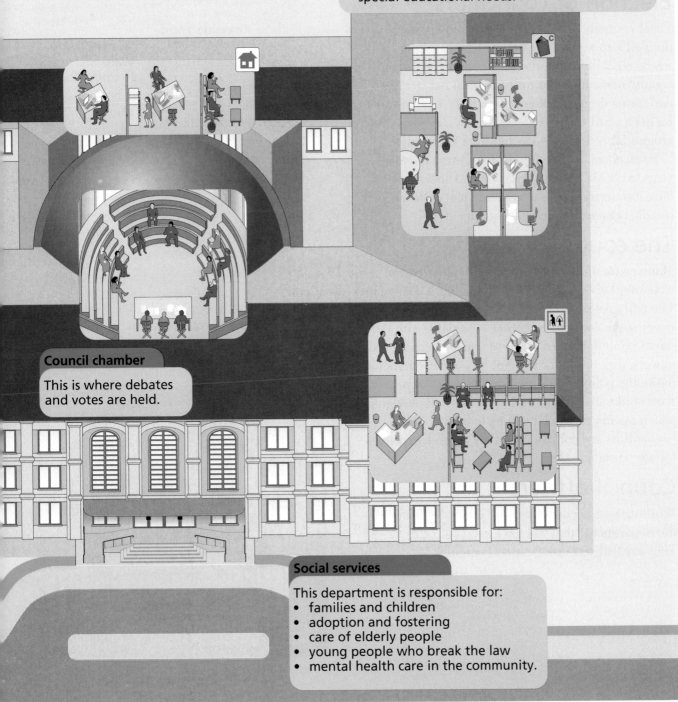

Housing

This department is responsible for:
- finding homes or accommodation for people who are homeless
- maintaining houses owned by the council
- services on council housing estates.

Education

This department:
- helps to run schools under the council's control
- gives money to schools in the borough
- helps sort out arrangements for children to go to school
- gives parents advice about schools
- has an education welfare section that handles truancy and arrangements for pupils with special educational needs.

Council chamber

This is where debates and votes are held.

Social services

This department is responsible for:
- families and children
- adoption and fostering
- care of elderly people
- young people who break the law
- mental health care in the community.

3.2 Who makes the decisions that affect your community?

The important decisions about what a council should do in an area are made by councillors. You are going to hold an election for a councillor and, as a class, you are going to play the people who want to be elected to the council. But first you need to know some more about councils.

Election of councillors

Local councils are elected. Each council area is divided into wards. The people who live in the wards elect the councillors. In country areas there is usually one councillor for each ward but in cities and towns there are often two or three councillors for each ward. A borough council in a city may have around 50 councillors elected from twenty wards.

Some councils have big elections every three or four years to choose a whole new council. Other councils have elections every year to choose part of the council, usually between a third and a quarter of it.

The council

Many councillors belong to a political party, for example, Labour, Conservative or Liberal Democrat. The party with the most councillors is in charge of running the council. Sometimes the party with the most councillors does not have a majority, so it has to work with other parties. Not all councillors belong to the big political parties. Some belong to smaller parties like the Greens and some are independent, which means they don't belong to a party at all. Councillors are not paid, but they receive expenses for attending meetings.

Council officers

Working for the councillors are council officers in the departments that you have seen on pages 42–43. They are full-time paid council officials.

Note: You can find out about the work of a councillor on Info page 60.

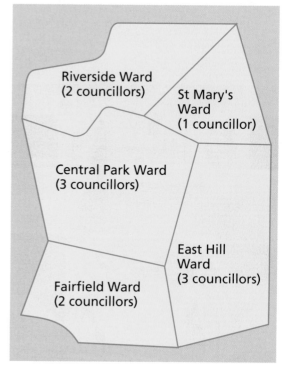

An example of council wards

Riverside Ward
(2 councillors)

St Mary's Ward
(1 councillor)

Central Park Ward
(3 councillors)

East Hill Ward
(3 councillors)

Fairfield Ward
(2 councillors)

A council chamber

Activity

1 Write out and complete sentences A–G by choosing from the definitions 1–7 listed below. You might need to look at page 60 to help you answer.

A A councillor is elected by the residents of a ward. A ward is ...

B A councillor can represent a political party or can be independent. **This means that he or she ...**

C A political party **is ...**

D The difference between a councillor and a council officer **is ...**

E Council decisions are made in a council chamber, **which is ...**

F The council decides how money will be spent locally. Some of this money comes from council tax, **which is ...**

G Most councillors hold surgeries, **which are ...**

1 ... the place in the town hall or council offices where all debates and votes on policy are held.

2 ... times in the week when a councillor can be consulted about a problem, at the councillor's office.

3 ... a geographical area within the boundaries of a local authority. Each ward has roughly the same number of residents.

4 ... paid to the local council by the residents of the area. The amount they pay is decided by the value of their home.

5 ... an organisation that stands for certain opinions and that some people support because they agree with these opinions.

6 ... does not belong to a political party and does not follow the opinions of any particular party.

7 ... a councillor is elected and votes on decisions in the local council; a council officer is paid to do a job and advises the councillor, but does not make decisions.

2 Do some research into the council in your area. Use your local library.
   a) What sort of council area do you live in? (Is it a borough or district council or something else?)
   b) Obtain a map of the council wards from your local council offices.
   c) Find out which ward you live in and who your councillors are.
   d) Find out when they have surgeries and when they meet local people.

3 Invite a councillor to come into school. The councillor could talk about his or her work and help you with the activities on pages 40–41 and 47.

3.3 Who will you vote for?

It is time for the local council to be elected (local elections take place on the first Thursday in May). A number of people want to get themselves elected on to the council for Trengarth, the town you can see in the drawing below. What problems can you see in Trengarth town centre that a councillor might want to do something about?

Now that you've looked at Trengarth's problems, it's time for the election campaign.

1 Campaign
Work in six groups of four or five people. Each group will be allocated one of the candidates on pages 48–49.
a) Decide who in the group will be the candidate. The other members of the group have to help the candidate prepare for the election.
b) What **policies** (plans) and arguments to support the candidate are you going to put forward?
c) Design and make a leaflet setting out why your candidate should be elected. Use a computer if possible.

2 Election meeting
The candidate from each group stands in the election. The rest of you are the voters.
   Each candidate should hand out their leaflet and make a five-minute presentation to say why they should be elected.

3 The vote

a) Ask your teacher for some copies of this ballot paper. Each voter will need one paper.

b) The voters should indicate their first and second choices by marking crosses in the appropriate boxes on the ballot paper.

c) Count up the crosses at the end. The overall winner is the candidate who got the most '1' votes. The candidate who came second is the one who got the most '1' and '2' votes added together.

Councillors for Riverside Ward	X VOTE ONCE IN EACH COLUMN	1st Choice	2nd Choice
1	HARDCASTLE, M.		
2	HARGREAVES, G.		
3	JACKSON, M.		
4	LEONARD, J.		
5	MANDELA, S.		
6	PATEL, N.		

4 After the vote, discuss these questions:

a) Did you give your vote to the candidate who had the best policies and put their case best?

b) Did you vote for the person you liked best because of their personality?

c) Did you vote for the candidate who came from your group?

d) Which candidate do you think had the best policies?

THE CANDIDATES

You are **N. Patel**. You have lived in the local community all your life, and are well known and respected. There are three issues that are close to your heart and which you want to base the campaign on:

■ improving existing housing estates
■ cleaning up the town centre
■ bringing more jobs into the area for young people.

Add any other local issues you wish to campaign on.

You are **J. Leonard** who has lived in the area for over ten years. You are a committed environmentalist. You are taking part in the election because of concern about one issue – the building of a road. This will mean:

• the demolition of two streets of houses
• an increase in the amount of traffic
• increased pollution
• the loss of some attractive common land with woods.

You want to stop the road being built. You are also concerned about other environmental issues, such as air and noise pollution, recycling and parkland.

You are **M. Hardcastle**. You moved into the area about three years ago and are an enterprising businessperson. You are very keen on developing the town centre to make it attractive for businesses. You want to:

• see the new road scheme go ahead because it will ease the pressure on the town centre, clear away some unattractive housing and reduce pollution in the centre
• pedestrianise part of the town centre
• persuade shopkeepers to invest in repainting and livening up the outside of their shops
• create jobs in the town.

Add any other local issues you wish to campaign on.

You are **S. MANDELA** and have lived in the area for over fifteen years. You want to see the area develop its sense of community. The areas you are interested in are:

- community centres for old people who are often on their own
- crèches and playgroups for babies and young children
- reducing crime
- improving local parks.

Add any other local issues you wish to campaign on.

You are **M. Jackson**, a new arrival in the area – a young enterprising person. You want to see the area livened up, particularly its entertainment facilities. You are interested in:

- licences for clubs
- a new cinema complex with six screens
- new shops in the high street
- cleaning up the streets in the town centre and introducing closed-circuit television cameras to reduce crime.

Add any other local issues you wish to campaign on.

You are **G. Hargreaves**, an older resident who has always lived in the area. You have served on the council before. You are anxious to see the area improve generally. Your main interests are:

- cutting down traffic and reducing noise and fumes
- getting rid of graffiti and litter in the streets
- improving local libraries and parks
- measures to reduce crime.

Add any other local issues you wish to campaign on.

3.4 Supermarket swoop!
A decision-making role play

Grantborough is a district in a small town. It has almost been swallowed up by the growing city of Lencaster nearby. It has a high street containing a newsagent and sweet shop, a small supermarket, a hardware store, a greengrocer, a hairdresser and a few other shops. The newsagent is also a sub post office. You can see what Grantborough looks like on the map.

There are not many jobs in the area, especially for young people and people who want part-time jobs. People have to travel into the city for work, or go further afield. The area is badly served by public transport, so the main way for people to get to work is by car. The roads are narrow and winding, and there is already traffic congestion in the mornings and evenings because commuters travel through Grantborough to reach the city. However, the area is attractive. There is a large park and the houses are low-level and pleasant.

Now a huge supermarket chain, Fairdeal, wants to build a large supermarket on a site not far from the high street. The site used to contain a shoe factory, but this has closed down. This is going to have a big effect on life in Grantborough and a number of people are worried about it. You can see the location of the proposed supermarket on the map.

To City of Lencaster

Dual carriageway

New housing estate

St John's church

Parkland

Housing

GRANTBOROUGH

Housing

Shops

Shops

Proposed supermarket site

Disused railway line siding

Housing

You are going to hold a public meeting about the new development.

1 Roles

a) Different groups in the local community have a variety of views on whether it is a good idea or not. Your class is going to divide into groups to play the roles of the people below:

- Supermarket developers, designers and public relations officers (this group should have at least five class members in it)
- Shopkeepers
- Parents with young children
- Residents' association
- Elderly people
- Environmentalists and conservationists
- Councillors.

b) On the next page you will find a brief for your group. Use the brief to work out your position on the new development. Do you welcome it or not? Or would you welcome it if the developers agreed to certain conditions about how the supermarket should be built?

2 The meeting

a) When you have thought about your position, hold a meeting to discuss the proposal. Your teacher, as the chairperson of a local residents' group, will be in charge of the meeting and ask people to speak in turn.

b) The meeting will start with the developers explaining how they intend to develop the supermarket. You will get the chance to ask the developers questions and to put your point of view. You might be able to persuade them to change the way they are going to develop the supermarket.

c) At the end of the meeting, take a vote to see if you want the supermarket or not.

3 Discuss the following issues as a class, if possible with an official from the planning office of your local council:

a) What effects do big developments like supermarkets have on communities? Think about the benefits as well as the disadvantages.

b) In what ways can local people make their voices heard when big developments take place in their area?

Group briefs

Supermarket developers, designers and public relations officers

You are anxious to develop a supermarket on this site. There is no space left in the city and people are increasingly shopping by car on the outskirts of cities. So, your task here is to sell the idea of the supermarket to the local people. You are able to make some changes according to what local people would like to see, but you know that some groups will still be against it. You just have to try and persuade them that it will bring them benefits.

Here are some of the ways in which you could appeal to them:

■ jobs, especially part-time ones that might particularly suit women with children. But there will also be full-time jobs in the warehouse and in management.

■ prices of goods

■ access roads

■ design of the supermarket to make it fit in with local environment, landscaping, measures to cut down noise

■ extra facilities – crèche, restaurant, free or cheap buses, etc.

Work out how you can use these factors. You might even draw a new design for the supermarket and the area around it.

Shopkeepers

You are very worried about the effects that the supermarket might have on your businesses. You need to:

■ think about how it might affect the prices of your goods and the number of your customers

■ find out what the supermarket owners are going to put in their new store. Are they going to have a full range of goods including, for example, clothes and newspapers?

Prepare a list of questions you want to put to the developers.

Councillors

You think that the supermarket will improve the amenities and services in Grantborough and bring money and jobs into the area. You think it is a good solution for the derelict factory site. But you are elected by the local people and don't want to upset them. You won't vote for the supermarket unless the developers give certain guarantees. Work out what you can ask them to do to improve the area and help the local people concerning:

■ a new access road to the supermarket. You want to solve the traffic problems caused by people driving into the city through Grantborough every day.

■ jobs

■ car parking facilities and toilets

■ environmental issues

■ local businesses.

Prepare questions that you want to ask the developers, particularly about the road.

Residents' association

Your group represents the residents – the people who live in Grantborough. You can see that the supermarket has advantages and disadvantages. The things that might worry you are:

- traffic
- what happens to local shops
- design of the supermarket – what it looks like and how it will fit in with other buildings
- access roads and car parking.

Work out your position. Prepare a list of questions you want to ask the developers and a list of things you would like to see them do to make the supermarket more acceptable to residents.

Elderly people

You represent elderly people who meet regularly at the local pensioners' club. You are very concerned about such a big change to the town. Work out:

- what your main worries and concerns are
- what the benefits of a supermarket would be to your age group
- what you would like to see the supermarket include to make it attractive to you.

Prepare a list of questions you want to ask the developers and a list of things you would like to see them do before you will support the proposal.

Environmentalists and conservationists

You are completely opposed to the supermarket development. There is nothing the developers can say to persuade you to change your mind. So you want to devise some difficult questions for them to answer and make some strong points against the development. Work out what you are going to say about:

- traffic – cars and delivery
- air and noise pollution
- the impact that the supermarket buildings will have on the look of Grantborough
- other damage to the environment
- loss of local shops and damage to the community.

Parents with young children

You have to work out whether this is going to be good for you or not. Some of the things you could discuss are:

- shopping (for example, easier or harder, range of goods available, prices)
- jobs
- getting to and from the supermarket
- problems of children on roads.

Prepare a list of questions you want to ask the developers and a list of things you would like to see them do before you will support the proposal.

Project 1: Make a guide for your local community

The things that affect us most are often the ones that are closest to us. The quality of our lives is affected by the services and amenities in our local area.

You are going to conduct a class survey of the services and amenities of the area around your school. At the end you are going to present a guide to the services in your area, so you have to think about who you are writing your guide for. It could be for people who have just arrived in your area or for use in a local library.

1 Decide what you want to find out about.

   a) Working in groups of four or five, brainstorm for five minutes your ideas about the services and amenities you want to include in your guide.

   b) Bring your ideas to the rest of the class and create a class list, for example:

   - leisure and entertainment (e.g. swimming pools, cinemas)
   - services for the elderly (e.g. lunch clubs)
   - libraries
   - services for children (e.g. nurseries)
   - voluntary organisations (e.g. the Samaritans).

   c) Decide on the boundaries of the area. Are you going to include the whole borough council or a smaller area around your school?

2 Stay in your groups of four or five. Decide on the kind of information you want to include in your guide:

   - Are you just going to put names and addresses?
   - Are you going to put other details, such as opening times and the costs of the services?

   - Are you going to put in some sort of comment on the organisation – what activities it offers, how it helps, if it offers special deals?

   Agree a class decision about this, so that everybody collects the same sort of information.

3 Make a list of places where you might find the information you want. Here are some ideas: parents and friends, library, Yellow Pages or local guides, the Town Hall, the internet (many councils have a website), local newspapers, Citizens' Advice Bureau.

4 Divide up the work between the different groups in the class. You can:

   - do different sections: for example, one group can concentrate on leisure and entertainment, while another looks at services for the elderly
   - get a sheet from your teacher to get you started.

5 Bring all your information together and produce your guide. Again you are going to have to share out the work. Perhaps the best way to do it is by computer.

   a) Set up some formatted page layouts with columns to enter the information. Then every group can take a turn at feeding in their information.

   b) Leave other pages for special reports on any local issues that you have come across.

   c) You could liven up your guide by taking photographs. See if you can get hold of a digital camera, then you can patch your photos directly into the guide.

   d) Design an exciting front cover using interesting typography (lettering) and a photo or illustration.

6 You may have found in your survey that some services and amenities were not available to local people. From what you have found out, discuss:

a) what services and amenities were missing

b) how existing services can be improved

c) what new amenities you would like to see in your local area.

7 You could invite a local councillor to talk about these issues, or write a class letter to the council telling them about your concerns and what you think could be done to improve your area.

Project 2: Get involved!

Your local council has a duty to provide good services. But you have a role to play in the community as well. You can contribute to your local community as an individual or as a class.

1 Identify a project

- If you have done Project 1, you will have come into contact with various organisations that serve the local community. This may have made you aware of how these organisations need help or need people to do things. Is there something that you or your class could usefully do? What needs have you identified?

- You could choose a specific organisation to work with: ask a representative to come into school to talk to you about its work.

- You may have become aware that certain services are missing from your local community. Are there any gaps you could plug?

2 Ideas for projects

If you have not done the services and amenities survey, you can still contact local voluntary organisations to find out how you could help. Here are some ideas:

- Do something for elderly people. For example, you could visit an old people's home to put on a play or you could interview them about life in the community in the past.

- Help on an environmental project. Contact local environmental groups for ideas.

- Run an event to support a local charity.

- Run some events for children's groups. You could set up a toy bank or toy exchange, where parents and children come in to borrow toys once a week.

- Help a local organisation. Invite representatives of several organisations to talk about their aims and objectives and what you could do to help.

3 Recording your project

Think about how you are going to record your community involvement. You could take photographs, make a video or write it all up and mount a huge display. The display could be placed in the local library or town hall.

Project 3: Make your own community newspaper

You know a lot about your local community. In your class you are going to write a community newspaper. You could get help on this from a local journalist. You may be able to visit a local newspaper office.

Look at these extracts from local newspapers. What kinds of issue are covered? Are they the same or different from the issues in your area? It would be helpful if you could bring some local newspapers into class.

Row kicks off over stadium's yes vote

News that Fulham Football Club can go ahead with its 30,000 seat riverside stadium has been welcomed by chairman Mohamed Al Fayed.

But many people in Putney are still angry, claiming Putney could pay the price of the club's good fortune.

Hundreds of placard-waving football fans packed into Hammersmith Town Hall last week for the decision.

Councillors thought the benefits of the scheme outweighed its problems. They have welcomed a promised new riverside walk and believe the new building will look better than the old stadium.

Many Putney people believe it will be a hugely dominant building that will ruin river views and sailing and cause traffic jams and parking problems both in Fulham and in Putney. Residents also fear hordes of football fans causing trouble on match days.

From the Wandsworth Borough Guardian, 8 March 2001

Scrawlers could be forced to wear pink
Councillor's bright idea for graffiti yobs

GRAFFITI vandals should be made to wear shocking pink overalls with "community offender" written on their backsides, says a Richmond councillor.

Douglas Orchard, an ex-miner and retired police sergeant, says public humiliation will do more to deter them than fines or even jail.

Cllr Orchard told the Informer: "I know from talking to youngsters that they detest community orders, because they restrict their social life at weekends.

"If we dressed the culprits in garish pink or something similar, with 'community offender' written on their butts, it would help resolve the problem."

"Once the culprits are named and shamed and made highly conspicuous while they clean off their filth in public, they will think twice about coming back for more punishment."

From the Richmond Informer, 28 April 2000

Meet Violet the kung fu rabbit

VIOLET the violent rabbit has been put in a solitary cell after she began launching kung-fu kicks on fellow bunnies.

Dawn Parkes, who helped rescue 1,152 rabbits from a vivisection clinic and regularly takes in new batches of bunnies, said she spotted Violet's brutal assaults on the other rabbits when she let a dozen of them loose in her garden.

She said: "Violet targets the rabbit she is after and then runs at them before jumping in the air, spinning round, and kicking them in the face with her back feet."

Mrs Parkes, of Catkin Close, High Wycombe, added: "I have called her Violent Violet because I have never seen this in a rabbit."

She has already homed seven rabbits but needs more people to come forward to give rabbits somewhere to live.

From the Bucks Free Press, 4 August 2000

End of the line for our rail users?

The people of Cornwall could be forgiven for thinking the train companies don't want their custom.

Complaints about lack of services, unpunctual trains and high cost of tickets are hardly unheard of, so it might have been imagined that the only way was up when it came to standard of service. Alas no.

This week the Association of Train Operating Companies revealed plans to only allow passengers to buy long distance tickets from the larger stations, not the likes of Bodmin Parkway, Liskeard or Par.

ATOC said it was trying to simplify the system and encouraging ticket sales over the internet.

MP Colin Breed has called the ticketing move "crass stupidity" and urged it to be opposed.

Of course, it should be, but just how is another matter.

From the *Cornish Guardian*, 10 August 2000

All change to homes and shops at Leadmill

This is the shape of the big housing, shops and workshops complex set to emerge from the ashes of the former Leadmill bus and tram depot in Sheffield's Cultural Industries Quarter.

Sheffield-based architects the Bond Bryan Partnership have been appointed to design the £13m development, which will become the home for around 450 students ready for next year's autumn term.

The distinctive twin turrets of the old garage will remain on the Shoreham Street site to be incorporated into the design of a new café-bar.

But most of the land will be redeveloped from scratch, creating the self-contained student flats, which Bond Bryan describe as a student village.

At the centre of the complex will be shops and workshop units, which it is thought will act as a catalyst for university-based start-up businesses.

The architects say they have designed three separate sites linked by new public thoroughfares.

Paul Cockerill, who is leading the development team, said: "By zoning a mix of complementary uses and placing emphasis on reinforcing the existing patterns of movement around and within the site, we aim to create exciting new urban spaces that will regenerate this once derelict area."

Earlier plans to redevelop the old bus and tram depot as The Music Garden, a complex of themed bars and a night club, were dropped after opposition from city licensing magistrates.

City councillors gave the go-ahead last month for the new project after being satisfied that changes had been made to protect residents from the noise of the nearby Leadmill nightclub.

From the *Sheffield Telegraph*, 1 September 2000

1 Discuss as a whole class which of the local issues that you have found out about might make good stories for the newspaper. These might include stories about local schools, crime, parks, graffiti, facilities for old people, animals – you decide.

2 When you have all agreed about the list of stories, you will need to decide who will be the editorial team (about four people) and who will be the journalists (the rest of the class).

The editorial team

Decide which group of journalists should write which story. You should write an editorial, which gives your opinion of a local subject. Look at the example from the *Cornish Guardian*, above left.

When the journalists have written their stories, your next job is to decide which stories should go where in the newspaper. You may also have to cut some of the journalists' stories to fit the paper and make changes to the journalists' headlines.

Journalists

a) Working in groups, you should write the story that you have been given by the editorial team.

b) Is there a photograph to go with the story? Can one be taken?

c) Discuss the angle (approach) of the story. Why would people be interested to read it?

d) Write the story – about 250 words. Make the first paragraph (about 75 words) exciting, so that people want to read on.

e) Decide on a good headline for the story.

f) Write a caption for the photograph.

g) When everyone in the group is happy with the story, type it into the computer.

h) Submit your story to the editorial team.

3 Produce your final newspaper on the computer and make photocopies. You could send one to all the people who helped you in your survey and during the community project.

3.6 What makes a 'good' citizen?

Politicians, newspaper editors and others tell us that schools should turn their pupils into good citizens. Of course this means **you!** You should become a 'good' citizen. The trouble is that it is not always easy to say exactly what a 'good' citizen is, and people don't always agree about it.

In this exercise you are going to discuss what you think it means to be a 'good' citizen and come up with your own ideas. Be careful: sometimes you have to distinguish between being 'good' and being a 'good citizen'. You might find it helpful to think about these points:

* Does a good citizen help other people?
* Does a good citizen always obey laws and rules?
* Is a good citizen someone who plays an active role in the community?

An active citizen

Some people think that taking an active part in your local community and in matters that affect the whole country is an important part of being a good citizen. Which of the statements above do you think are about being an active citizen who gets involved?

Activity

In this activity you are going to try to work out what a 'good' citizen might be. The statements on the right will help you do this. Work in twos or threes.

1 Decide which of the statements you agree with, which of them you don't agree with and which you can't decide about. Draw up a chart like the one below and put each statement in one of the columns.

Agree	Disagree	Can't decide

2 Make a list of your top five statements – the ones you think are most important for a good citizen to do or be. If you wish, you can add to or change the statements before adding them to your list.
3 Add two more statements of your own about how a good citizen should behave.
4 As a whole class, discuss:
   a) which statements you found it difficult to decide about and why
   b) which ones you didn't agree with
   c) which ones you did agree with
   d) the extra statements that different groups added to the list
   e) what your idea of a 'good' citizen is now.
5 Decide as a class on a top ten list.
6 Again in groups, choose one item from the list and design a poster about it to encourage other young people to be active citizens. Explain your ideas to the rest of the class.

A votes in elections to choose who should run the country (national government).

B never drops litter on the streets.

C takes part in local campaigns (for example, joins others in blocking the road to demand that a new zebra crossing is built).

D watches the neighbours very closely to make sure they are not up to mischief.

E reports neighbours to the local authority if they are noisy or litter the streets.

A 'Good' Citizen...?

F never has parties in case the noise disturbs the neighbours.

G tells people off for dropping litter or letting their dogs foul the street.

H obeys all laws and rules at all times.

I stays out late at night having a good time with friends.

J takes newspapers and bottles to the recycling centre.

K works for a local charity.

L has strong religious beliefs and goes to church/synagogue/holy place regularly.

M takes part in election campaigns by distributing leaflets for a political party.

N takes strong action over important issues (for example, where a road is being built through a beauty spot) even if this means breaking the law.

O does not write graffiti on walls.

P reports vandals to the police.

Q takes part in a neighbourhood watch group to stop criminals.

R is pleasant to people if they ask for help (for example, giving directions).

S takes books back to the library on time.

T votes in elections to choose who should run the council (local government).

U helps elderly neighbours and pops round to check they are OK.

3.7 Councillors and councils

Who can become a councillor?

You must be at least 21 years old and live in the area of the council you want to be on. Some categories of people, such as many council employees, are not allowed to stand for election to the council.

How can you become a councillor?

You become a candidate for a ward (see page 44). In some councils, such as district councils, there is usually one councillor per ward, but in city wards there may be two or three.

All local elections take place on the first Thursday in May. Councillors are elected to serve for four years. Local elections use the first-past-the-post system. This means that the candidate with the highest number of votes wins. In wards that have three councillors to represent them, the three with the highest number of votes are elected.

The council

All the elected councillors and some senior council officers meet around once a month to discuss issues affecting the local area and to decide what to do about them.

Committees

Most of the detailed work is done in council committees. A small number of councillors sit on a committee, which overlooks the work of a particular department and decides the policy of the department. Council officers also sit on the committee to give information and advice. For example, the Planning Committee makes decisions about which housing developments should be allowed to go ahead. Some very important decisions have to go back to full council.

What work does a councillor do?

Meeting local people

Councillors hold surgeries, where local people can go to discuss their problems with their councillor. These might include problems on their housing estate, dirty streets or the lack of nurseries in the area.

section 4

Central government and Parliament
Who's running the country?

Key words
- monarchy
- democracy
- government
- Parliament
- election
- Member of Parliament
- Prime Minister

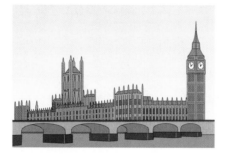

Local government is needed to provide services and manage the areas where we live. We also need a government to manage the whole country – a national government. Imagine what it would be like if different parts of the United Kingdom had different laws. You might be able to drive a car at the age of 15 in one part of the country, but not until 20 in another part. Some parts of the country might decide to use different money instead of pounds and pence. Criminals might be able to cross over borders and escape justice. So we need a government to make decisions about laws that we must all obey.

We also need a national government to speak for the whole country. This is particularly important when we trade with other countries or when we are involved in arguments with other countries. We need a national government to defend the country in time of war and to make decisions about helping other countries to keep the peace.

The British system of government has developed over centuries. It is a *parliamentary* system. The people elect Members of Parliament to represent our views in Parliament. The political party that has most MPs forms the government. We can throw the government out at the next election if we do not like what it is doing. We say this is a *democratic* system.

In this section you will find out about:

* how the British Parliament works
* what happens in the House of Commons
* making laws
* the job of a Member of Parliament.

You will:

* work with others
* argue a case
* give your opinion and explain it to others.

You can find out more about Planet Hoff on pages 2–3, 18–19, and 90–91.

HOFF
GOVERNMENT

S-L3

S-L3

S-L3

THE GOVERNMENT ZONE

As a member of the United Council for Galactic Trade's team of investigators, you have already visited Planet Hoff in sections 1 and 2. This time your team is looking at the way the planet is governed – who makes the decisions and who makes the laws that the inhabitants of the planet have to obey. You can find a description of the different groups who live on the planet on pages 18–19.

The government of Hoff

The Sesar

The planet is ruled by a Sesar, also called the Great One. She lives in a huge palace. All over the planet there are pictures and statues of the Great One. The religion of the Planet Hoff says that the Sesar is chosen by the Great Spirit and is the true leader who must be obeyed.

The Sesar makes all the big decisions about what happens on the planet. She has the power of life and death. She can order the execution of anyone who criticises her or who does not carry out her orders. She also makes all the laws. But Hoff is a big planet and the Sesar cannot run it all on her own. She has an organisation or government to help her. The most important members of the government are Uppers.

Ministers

The different parts of the government, or departments, are run by Uppers called Ministers. Their departments are:

* Relations with Other Planets
* Internal Affairs (law and order on the planet)
* Education and Health
* Food Supply
* Trade and Manufacture.

The Ministers meet with the Sesar once every moon period. They tell her what their policies (plans) are; if she agrees, they can put their policies into action. For instance, the Minister of Food Supply is putting into action a policy to grow more food. He wants to build a dam on the Blue River, so that citizens of Hoff have more water to irrigate the fields. The Sesar has agreed and the dam will be built. However, she does not always agree. When the Minister of Education wanted the citizens of Hoff to be able to read books from other planets, the Sesar did not think it was a good idea.

Each of the Ministers has a department in its own building. The citizens who work in these buildings are Thinkers. Their job is to carry out the decisions made by the Ministers and the Sesar. They draw up rules and regulations. They send out instructions to schools, builders, farmers, traders and others telling them what they should do and what rules they should follow.

The Secrocops

The Secrocops are a part of the government that the Hoffs don't talk about much. They are a secret police force run by the Minister of Internal Affairs. They search out people who break the law or who criticise the Sesar and her government. These people are put on trial and are always found guilty. Then they are sent to one of the two moons that go round Hoff, where they work as slave labourers in the crystal mines.

Ordinary citizens

Ordinary citizens of Hoff – Capitos, Doers, Gronks and most Thinkers – have no say in the way they are ruled. No one asks their opinions or cares what they think. For instance, 3,000 Doers will have to leave the area where they live and farm when the dam project goes ahead. This has made some of them very rebellious and they have organised resistance to the Sesar.

But most Hoffs do as they are told and don't cause any trouble. Some are frightened by what will happen to them if they speak out against the government. Many of the others, especially the Capitos, like the system of government because decisions are made quickly and things get done quickly. They never get any trouble from the Doers who work for them because they are too frightened to say anything.

Activity

1 **Draw and complete a copy of the outline chart below to show how the Hoff system of government works.**

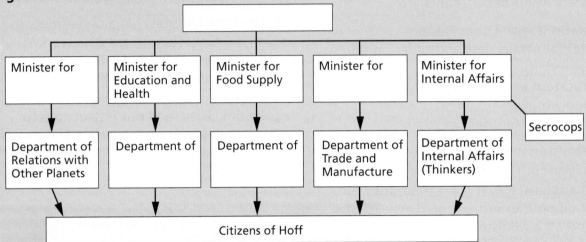

2 **Use colours on your diagram to show who has most power, who has power over whom, and who has least power. For example, those with most power could be marked in red.**

3 **What do you think the different groups on Hoff might feel about the system of government? Match a speech bubble with each of the following groups:**
   a) **Uppers, including the Sesar and her Ministers**
   b) **Thinkers**
   c) **Capitos**
   d) **Doers**
   e) **Gronks**

A I must do as I'm told. If I don't, my masters will be angry and I will be punished.

B The Sesar is a strong leader. She helps our businesses to do well. Anyone who opposes her is a troublemaker and should be handed over to the Secrocops.

C We know what is best for our planet. We are in touch with the Great Spirit. It is our duty to lead those who are below us.

D We are well educated and do most of the important jobs on this planet. We do not always agree with our leaders and it is time our views were listened to.

E Our employers just want us to work hard and never ask any questions.

4 **Which groups do you think would be most in favour of the system of government and which groups do you think would feel unfairly treated?**

5 **What do you think are the advantages and disadvantages of a system of government like the one on Planet Hoff?**

Note: Don't think that humans have never had systems of government like the one on Hoff. Russia in the nineteenth century had a ruler called a Tsar who took the decisions and made the laws. He had ministers to help him and a secret police. The people had no say in the government and could not choose who they wanted to rule them. People who criticised the Tsar were put in prison or sent into exile. We call this sort of system an autocracy.

Can you work out how the United Kingdom is governed?

A country needs a government to make decisions and get things done. These might be decisions about building roads and hospitals, how public transport can be improved, whether the army should help keep the peace in other countries, or how poorer parts of the country can be helped. The government has to collect money – taxes – to pay for all the things it does and the services it provides, such as the National Health Service. Then it has to decide how to spend the money.

The UK used to be a monarchy – it was run by a king or a queen. The monarch made all the decisions and people had to obey the king or queen or suffer the consequences. But the British people did not think this was a fair system of government. They wanted someone to speak for them, or *represent* their views, in a Parliament (talking place).

To start with, the British Parliament mostly gave advice to the monarch. But over several centuries it became more and more powerful, while the monarch became much weaker. Today we have what is called a *parliamentary* system of government.

Activity

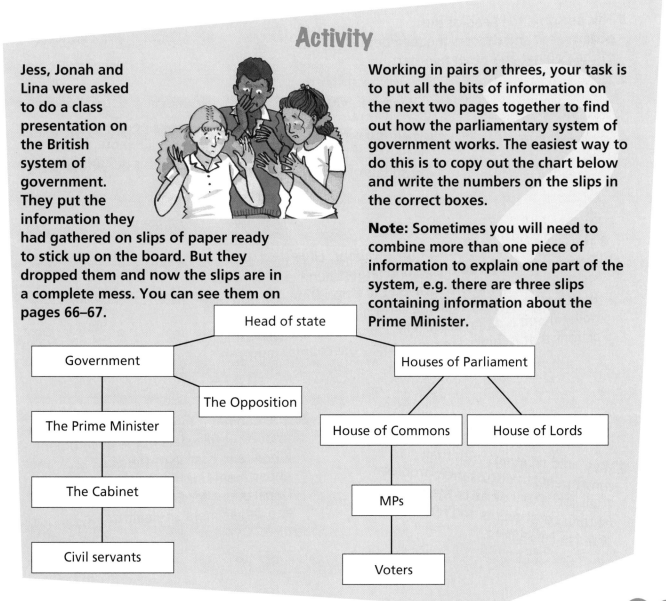

Jess, Jonah and Lina were asked to do a class presentation on the British system of government. They put the information they had gathered on slips of paper ready to stick up on the board. But they dropped them and now the slips are in a complete mess. You can see them on pages 66–67.

Working in pairs or threes, your task is to put all the bits of information on the next two pages together to find out how the parliamentary system of government works. The easiest way to do this is to copy out the chart below and write the numbers on the slips in the correct boxes.

Note: Sometimes you will need to combine more than one piece of information to explain one part of the system, e.g. there are three slips containing information about the Prime Minister.

- Head of state
- Government
- The Opposition
- Houses of Parliament
- The Prime Minister
- House of Commons
- House of Lords
- The Cabinet
- MPs
- Civil servants
- Voters

1 The monarch is the 'head of state' and entertains important foreign visitors. The king or queen opens and closes Parliament, but now has no real power and takes little part in government.

2 There are two Houses of Parliament – the House of Commons and the House of Lords.

4 The House of Commons is made up of 659 MPs.

3 Civil servants work for the government.

6 They discuss and vote on new laws.

5 This person is the head of the government and chooses the members of the Cabinet and other ministers.

7 Their job is to carry out the government's policies. For instance, if the government decides to build more hospitals or more roads, they make sure this is done.

8 The political party (Conservative, Labour, Liberal Democrat) which has the second largest number of MPs in the House of Commons is called the Opposition. The job of the Opposition is to examine carefully what the government is doing and challenge government plans and actions that it thinks are going to do the country harm.

10 The Cabinet is made up of the most important ministers in the government, who are in charge of the big departments such as the Home Office, Department for Education and Skills, and Department of Health.

9 They hold meetings with their constituents to discuss their problems. Their job is to look after the interests of their constituents and represent them in Parliament.

11 They hold debates on important issues in the House of Commons.

12 This group of people works with the Prime Minister to decide the government's major policies: for instance, what it is going to do about schools, keeping law and order, and running the health service.

13 The House of Lords is made up of peers (people who have titles), important judges and archbishops and bishops in the Church of England. Some of the peers inherited their titles; some were given them as rewards. This House is changing.

15 Members of Parliament (MPs) are elected by the people who live in a particular area or constituency in the town or country.

14 The Prime Minister is the first minister. He or she is the leader of the largest party (the one with most MPs) in the House of Commons.

16 This person is head of the armed forces, recommends appointments of senior judges and archbishops, and is in charge of relations with other countries.

17 The government is formed by the political party (e.g. Labour, Conservative, Liberal Democrat) that wins the general election. This is the party that has the most MPs in the House of Commons.

18 The voters (or electorate) are British people over 18 years old who have the right to vote in elections. Members of the House of Lords, mental patients in institutions, and prisoners serving sentences over 12 months are not allowed to vote.

19 The job of this House is to check the laws being made by the House of Commons. If they don't agree with a new law that is coming through, they can try to change it.

Discuss

What are the main differences between the British system of government and that on Planet Hoff?

The Prime Minister and the other members of the government run the United Kingdom. But they can't do just what they want. They have to explain and account for their actions in the House of Commons. They can be questioned and challenged by MPs to explain their actions.

The government needs the support of the House of Commons. If a majority of MPs in the House regularly vote against the government, it may have to resign and hold a new election.

Activity

Copy the outline drawing of the inside of the House of Commons. Then decide where the people below sit in the House and put them in the correct position on your drawing. Use the information boxes below to work out where they sit. Be careful: one of them isn't allowed to sit in the House of Commons.

The monarch
who is the head of state

The Prime Minister
who is the head of the government

Leader of the Opposition
who is the leader of the second largest party

- The Speaker sits in the Speaker's chair at the end of the Commons behind the table and dispatch box.

The Speaker
who is the chairperson of the House of Commons. He or she organises debates, chooses speakers and keeps order during debates.

Government ministers
who work with the Prime Minister to run the country

- The government and the Opposition sit facing one another.

- The Prime Minister stands at the dispatch box to make announcements or answer questions.

- Government ministers sit on the front benches on the right of the Speaker.

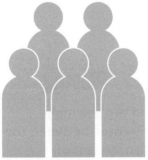

Back-benchers
who support the government

Back-benchers
who oppose the government

What work does the House of Commons do?

- It makes laws.
- It controls the money that the government spends.
- It questions the government and examines what it is doing.
- It holds debates on issues of national importance.

Do you know...

- the name of the Prime Minister?
- the name of the Leader of the Opposition?
- the name of the Speaker?
- the names of some members of the government?

- The Opposition leaders sit on the front benches opposite the government.

- The Opposition back-benchers are on the left of the Speaker.

- The back-benchers supporting the government sit behind the government ministers.

- The king or queen is not allowed inside the House of Commons.

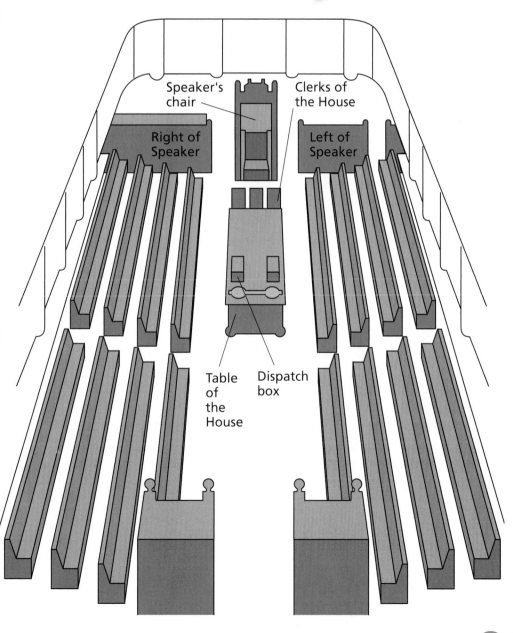

Speaker's chair

Clerks of the House

Right of Speaker

Left of Speaker

Table of the House

Dispatch box

4.4 How does Parliament make laws?

A case study: should smacking children be made illegal?

One of the main jobs of the House of Commons is to pass new laws, change ones that already exist and get rid of ones that no longer serve any useful purpose.

How a law is passed

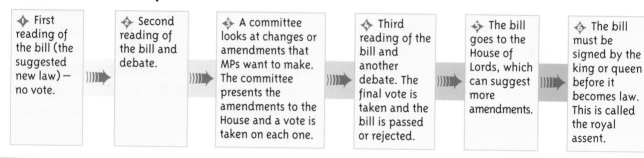

❖ First reading of the bill (the suggested new law) – no vote.

❖ Second reading of the bill and debate.

❖ A committee looks at changes or amendments that MPs want to make. The committee presents the amendments to the House and a vote is taken on each one.

❖ Third reading of the bill and another debate. The final vote is taken and the bill is passed or rejected.

❖ The bill goes to the House of Lords, which can suggest more amendments.

❖ The bill must be signed by the king or queen before it becomes law. This is called the royal assent.

Activity

Work in groups of three. You are going to make a new law about the physical punishment of children. You have to follow the rules below.

1 The new bill proposes that **parents should not be able to hit their children under any circumstances.** You are going to debate the bill in class (see the rules of debate on page 16).
2 The class must divide into two halves, one half supporting the bill and the other half opposing it. This means that you may have to argue for something that you do not believe. It is important to do this sometimes, so that you can see that people on the other side of an argument have a point of view, and so that you can construct a case using reasons and supporting evidence rather than emotional arguments.
3 First, work in your small group. Use some of the statements on pages 70–71 as well as your own ideas to develop your argument. Choose which one of your group is going to speak in the debate. This means that there should be three or four speakers for each side.
4 Hold the debate.
5 Each group of three can now suggest one amendment (change) to the bill that they think is fair and good. The whole class votes on these amendments. If there is a majority in favour of an amendment, it is passed.
6 The class now votes on the whole bill, including the agreed amendments. If the majority vote for it, the teacher signs it and it becomes law.

A There's never a good reason for smacking a child.

B It's better to spend time talking to a child if he or she has done something wrong.

C If they have hit someone else, it's important for them to find out what it's like to be hit.

D If you allow people to smack a child, some adults will always go too far and hit the child too hard.

E A short, sharp smack corrects a small child much more quickly than hours of talking. They soon learn what's right or wrong.

F Small children don't understand what is said to them.

G I've been smacked and it certainly did me no harm.

H If you smack children a lot, what they learn is that you get your way by being violent.

I The only way we can be sure that parents don't hit children too hard is to stop them hitting children altogether.

J Children who are hit often grow up to be adults who hit their children a lot.

K Children should have the same rights as adults. You wouldn't hit an adult if they made too much noise or ran around. So you shouldn't hit a child either.

L There are better ways to control children than to hit them.

4.5 What does an MP do?

Members of Parliament (MPs) are elected to the House of Commons. The people who vote for an MP live in a particular area of the country called a constituency. The average number of people in a constituency is around 67,000. It is the job of the MP to represent all of the people who live in their constituency. These people are called constituents.

Dr Jenny Tonge is the Liberal Democrat MP for Richmond Park constituency and front-bench Shadow Secretary of State for International Development. She was elected to the House of Commons in 1997. She had been a local councillor in Richmond-upon-Thames for ten years. She is a qualified doctor who has worked in the National Health Service and she has three grown-up children.

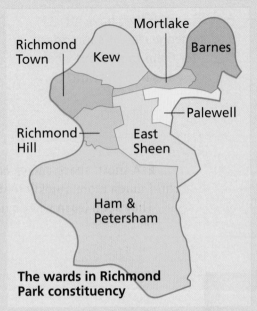

The wards in Richmond Park constituency

What does Jenny Tonge do as an MP?

In her constituency
- Holds surgeries where people can talk about their concerns or problems
- Visits schools, hospitals and day centres
- Listens to constituents' views, receives and answers letters

In the House of Commons
- Represents her party on various committees
- Takes part in debates
- Makes speeches
- Asks the government questions
- Raises issues important to people in the constituency

Travelling
- Makes speeches on behalf of her party in different parts of the country
- Finds out more about particular issues in the UK and abroad

Dr Jenny Tonge MP

What do you like about the job?

What I like about being an MP is the variety of the topics we deal with. Anything from the position of Muslim women in Kosovo to housing problems in Richmond. The range is absolutely fantastic; you never know what is going to happen.

You have to know that things can change and that you can make a difference. Quite often you don't do that in the House of Commons chamber. You do it by meeting ministers or groups of people in the background before the bill is even tabled. And there are a lot of personal things for constituents that you can change as an MP. There is no doubt that an MP's influence can help tremendously to sort out a problem.

What kinds of things do people ask you about at your surgery?

A lot are about people getting a raw deal in some way, often to do with housing or money in one form or another. People will also come when they have a complaint about a school or a hospital, or not getting their child into a particular school. Student grants have been causing an awful lot of problems recently. Because there are some people who are being very badly affected by not having a grant and having to find tuition fees.

One of the biggest issues in the last eighteen months has been asylum seekers. There's been a huge delay in the immigration department, so people come to the local MP to see if they can speed things up. Some delays have been going on for years and the situation some people are in really is pathetic.

I also see groups of people who have got together. I was in school last Friday and some of the young people there, in years 8 and 9, were beefing about the lack of leisure facilities in the area and the sorts of thing they wanted. So I've asked them to get together, decide what they want, present me with a few suggestions and a petition, and I will help them go to the right people and try and see if we can do something about that.

So what sorts of thing are you able to do for people who come to the surgery?

I can put people on to the council, or I can write a letter, or I can blast a particular officer and say 'get on and sort this one out'. And the same for national departments, the Child Support Agency, the Pensions Agency, the Immigration Department. A blast from an MP counts a bit more than a blast from an ordinary person, unfortunately.

How much of your time is spent in the House of Commons?

Actually sitting in the House of Commons chamber is probably very low down on the list when it comes to the amount of time spent on things. People like to go to Question Time (which happens every afternoon). If it's in your particular area, you might be the main questioner for your party. It's also crucial to be there at voting time, which is always the end of the evening – it's usually 10 o'clock, but recently we have had 72 nights since Christmas when it's been after midnight.

The other time you are in the House of Commons is when there is a debate which concerns your area of expertise. For instance, last week I was very lucky to secure a debate from the Speaker on health services in London which, because I was a doctor before I was an MP, I was interested in.

I also spend a lot of time working on committees. Some of these look closely at bills and make amendments to them before they become laws. Other committees look carefully at what the government is doing about certain big issues like the debt of Third World countries.

Do you like being an MP?

I just love it! **C**

Discuss

1 Which parts of Jenny Tonge's job would you particularly enjoy? Why?
2 Which parts would you not enjoy?
3 What characteristics do you think a person would need to be a good MP?

Activity

Use your local library to find out:
a) who your MP is
b) the name of the constituency in which you live
c) when you could meet your MP.

Write to your MP

Letter 1

3 Station Road
Grimsditch
Midshire
15 April

James Winston MP
House of Commons
London
SW1A 0AA

Dear Mr Winston,

I'm really sick about a new supermarket being built in my town. It is going to be really ugly. The council isn't bothered and don't answer my letters. I want it stopped and so do all the people I know. I want you to do something about it.

Yours sincerely,

Janet Johnson

Activity

1 MPs receive a lot of letters. Some of them are well written and argue their case well, but some are not as good. Look at the two letters on this page. Decide which is better and say why.

2 Write a letter to, or e-mail, your MP. In your other citizenship work, you have probably come across an issue you feel strongly about. This might be the environment or some development schemes in your local area; it might have to do with schools. In your letter, explain your views or ideas and ask for the MP's reaction.

Letter 2

3 Station Road
Grimsditch
Midshire
15 April

James Winston MP
House of Commons
London
SW1A 0AA

Dear Mr Winston,

I am writing about the plans for a large new supermarket on the outskirts of our town. The council seems to be on the side of the developers and won't help us. We have collected a petition with over three thousand signatures of people who do not think we need another supermarket in Grimsditch.

The shops in the town centre will lose trade if this goes ahead. Traffic will increase through the town and more trolleys will be abandoned. Jobs will be lost in the town as a result of some small shops closing and the town centre will die as it has done in lots of other towns. The heart will be ripped out of our community. Our town may be called Grimsditch but it is really a very attractive place and we don't want to see it become empty and deserted.

I hope that you will be able to persuade the council to stop the development.

Yours sincerely,

Janet Johnson

4.6 Democracy – British style

Who can stand as a candidate in a general election?

Any person over 21 years old who is a British or Commonwealth citizen, except:

* members of the House of Lords
* clergy
* bankrupts
* prisoners sentenced to more than one year in prison
* people suffering from certain mental health conditions
* people who have certain jobs (for example, judges, members of regular armed forces and police officers, who should not take political sides in their jobs).

Who is able to vote in parliamentary elections?

All British citizens over 18 years old can vote except:

* members of the House of Lords
* prisoners sentenced to more than one year in prison
* patients held under mental health laws
* people convicted within the previous five years of corrupt or illegal practices during elections.

Voting is not compulsory.

What is a constituency?

The United Kingdom is divided up into areas called constituencies. You live in a constituency and this is the area you vote in. You can vote for one person to represent you in Parliament – Member of Parliament (MP). Most candidates in general elections are put forward by political parties, and by voting for one of them you are also voting for the party you wish to be in government. The average size of a constituency is around 67,000 people.

How often do we have general elections?

The maximum life of a government is five years. So there has to be an election at least every five years. But a Prime Minister can call an election at any time during those five years, so you could have an election after three or four years. It is for the Prime Minister to decide this, but he or she will usually discuss it with the government's ministers and other people in the party.

What happens when the Prime Minister decides to call a general election?

The Prime Minister goes to the monarch to request that Parliament be dissolved (brought to an end). A Royal Proclamation is issued which allows the dissolution (ending) of Parliament. General elections are usually held 17 days after this.

What does the monarch do?

The king or queen is the head of state. The monarch was very powerful in the past, but is not now. The main role of the monarch in our parliamentary system is to:

* open and close Parliament
* ask the leader of the party with the most MPs after an election to become Prime Minister and form a government
* give the royal assent to new laws
* meet leaders and heads of state from other countries
* give out honours to people who have given noteworthy public service.

It is not quite clear exactly how powerful the monarch is. For instance, the queen could refuse to sign new laws; then they could not be put into action. In times of crisis or emergency, the monarch could play an important role if there was something wrong with the government.

The House of Commons and the House of Lords

The British Parliament is a two-house system. The House of Commons is the house that has the most power. This is because its members are elected by the people and the MPs represent the views of the people. The government is chosen from the political party that has the largest number of MPs.

The main work of the House of Commons includes:

* making laws
* controlling the amount of money that the government spends and is able to take from the people in taxes
* examining closely the work of the government by asking questions, having debates and having committees to look closely at particular areas of government work. This is to make sure that the government is working in the interests of the people. It stops governments becoming too powerful or corrupt: for example, giving favours to the people who support it.

The second house, the House of Lords, is there as a safety check:

* to make sure that the House of Commons does not rush through new laws that are not very good
* to criticise the government if it thinks that government has become too powerful.

The main work of the House of Lords includes:

* being part of making laws
* examining the work of government, asking questions, holding debates on proposed laws, and having committees
* holding general debates on important issues (for example, is it right to use animals in experiments?).

How are laws made in Parliament?

While a proposal for a new law is going through Parliament, before it becomes a law, it is called a bill. The bill has to be properly drafted (written out), explaining carefully how and when the new law is going to be used. Parliament can reject bills that it thinks will not be good for the people of the UK.

Stages in making a law

1 First reading. The bill is introduced to Parliament in the House of Commons. It is published for MPs to read. There is no discussion or vote.

2 Second reading. A government minister explains the purpose of the bill and answers questions about it. Only if a majority of MPs vote for the bill can it go on to the next stage.

3 Committee stage. A committee of between 16 and 60 MPs looks at the details of the bill and discusses them. This may take weeks or months. Committee members may suggest changes or amendments to the bill. The committee votes for or against the amendments.

4 Report stage. The whole House of Commons hears about what has happened in the committee and MPs can suggest further changes.

5 Third reading. This gives the House of Commons a chance to look at the whole bill again with all its amendments. The bill cannot be changed much at this stage. It is either accepted (MPs vote for it) or rejected (MPs vote against it).

6 House of Lords. The bill goes to the House of Lords, which checks it. It goes through similar stages to those in the House of Commons. The Lords can suggest more changes to the bill and there may be some discussion with the House of Commons about these. But although the House of Lords may delay a bill and therefore cause difficulties for the government, it cannot stop a bill going through.

7 Royal assent. Once the bill has been passed by both Houses, it goes to the monarch. The monarch has to sign papers agreeing to the bill. The royal assent (agreement) is then read out in the House of Lords.

8 Act of Parliament. The bill is now a law. It may have taken several months to go through all the stages. But if there is an urgent need, a bill can go through in a matter of days or even hours.

section 5

The media and society
How do you find out what's going on?

Key words
- media
- censorship
- images
- fact
- opinion

Everyone is affected by mass media these days. The media are: television, radio, newspapers, magazines, films, advertising, popular music and the internet. All of these are different forms of communication and they reach millions of people. Through them we hear about the news, fashion, current events, entertainment, celebrities and new products. We spend a great deal of our time and our money on the media. The media influence what we think, how we dress, what we spend our money on, how we vote, what we eat, what we know – the list is endless. Many people think that the media have too much influence. We need to be aware of how the media persuade us to adopt certain views or buy particular goods.

The media also do another important job: they tell us what the government is doing and help to expose any wrongdoing by the government, by big companies or by other people. This is important. It helps keep our society 'free' because we can challenge powerful people. Governments in some countries try to control the media because they do not want people to criticise them or challenge what they are doing. We call this censorship.

In this section, you will learn about:

* the different forms of mass media
* how the different parts of the media influence people
* what we learn from the media
* thinking for ourselves.

You will:

* find out about the way the media work
* analyse examples of the media
* discuss the media in small groups and as a whole class
* make decisions
* give your opinion and explain it to others
* listen to other people's opinions.

5.1 Your media diary

Here is the media diary of a 13-year-old, Alex.

7.00a.m.	Wake up when clock-radio goes off – tuned to Radio 1.
7.10a.m.	Shower and dress.
7.30a.m.	Watch *The Big Breakfast* while eating breakfast.
8.00a.m.	Bus to school reading computer magazine. Spot an ad for a new game for my PC – to put on the birthday presents list.
8.40a.m.	Arrive at school and listen to music on headphones until registration.
4.30p.m.	Arrive home and flick through the Sun to see what is on television this evening.
5.00p.m.	Eat tea.
5.30p.m.	Watch *Neighbours*.
6.00p.m.	Phone call from friend who suggests going to the cinema.
6.10p.m.	Rush homework using internet, and meet friend.
7.00p.m.	Watch latest sci-fi movie which was great – brilliant new advertisement for jeans before the film.
9.30p.m.	Home to finish homework.
11.00p.m.	Go to bed and watch MTV.

Activity

1 Write a diary of a day in your life, naming all the different media you look at or listen to in an average day.
2 For how many hours in a normal day do you have some contact with the media?
3 Draw up and carry out a survey of another tutor/form group to find out what media they look at or listen to during a typical day, how long they watch television, listen to the radio and so on.

What do we learn from the media?

Activity

1 Look at the following list of things we learn and hear about from the media. Working in small groups, decide which examples of media would tell us about each of these things. Write the lists on a copy of the chart.

What we learn	Which media
Up-to-date news and current affairs	TV news and documentaries, radio, newspapers
Gossip about celebrities	
Information about new products on the market	
Political opinions	
Sports	
Local news and events	
Information about popular music	
Attitudes towards particular products and brands	
Information about stocks and shares	
Educational topics	
Latest fashions in clothes	

2 Give some examples of any other things we learn from the media and where we would read, see or hear about them.

5.2 Can you trust an advert?

The purpose of advertising is to sell products or to bring information to our attention. Sometimes the aim is to tell people that a new product is available, where it can be bought and how much it will cost. But usually, people already know about products. The advertisers want to persuade us to buy a particular brand of product, such as Nike trainers or Cadbury's chocolate.

Advertisers use many different techniques to persuade us to buy their products.

Advertising techniques

Appeal to snobbery	The message is that only rich, important people with good taste buy this product.
Sex appeal	Beautiful, young, sexy people are shown using the product. The message is – 'you too could be like this, if you buy the product'.
Use of humour	The advert makes people laugh, so they feel good about the product.
Quirky images and words	It is not always clear what these adverts are saying. People spend time trying to figure them out. The brand name sticks.
Shock tactics	The advert uses images which grab people's attention. The brand name sticks.
Targeting an audience	An advert is placed where it will appeal to a particular group of people (for example, young people interested in fashion).
Use of celebrities	Famous people are shown using the product. The message is that it must be a good product if people we admire use it.
Use of guilt	The advert makes people worry that they are not doing the right thing if they don't follow the advice in the advert.

Activity

1 Look at the techniques in the chart on the left. Decide which is being used in each of these advertisements.
2 List as many adverts as you can that use these techniques.
3 Bring in your own collection of different sorts of magazine. Cut out and make a collage of adverts that use different techniques to persuade you to buy something or join something.

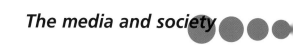

Hey mom, I'm home! [open the box] I'm *starving*.

[tear off a Ball Park Single] What do we have to eat?

[pop it in the microwave] Seriously, mom. If I don't

have something **right now I'll faint!** [ding!]

[it's ready] Mmmmmmmmm. *Thanks mom!*

Ball Park Singles.

The big, juicy taste steams right in, in only
about 40 seconds. There's no faster, easier w

Before we treat your tastebuds,
we treat the cows.

It's what goes into it that
makes it taste so good.

At Yeo Valley Organic, not only do the cows get to graze on the finest, lush, organic grass, they also enjoy a spacious barn fitted
with soft matting to bed down on. Why? Because we believe the happier the cows, the better their milk. But that's not
our only secret. We also insist on using naturally ripened organic fruit, which provides us with natural flavour and sugar. Then we
gently stir our yogurt to keep it smooth and creamy. Why not grab a spoon and try some. It goes down a treat.

www.yeo-organic.co.uk

I Want To Have All Three...

Listening to TEAC can
seriously damage your
single status.

Because, with the intro-
duction of the new
Reference 100, there are
now three Reference
Series Systems to choose
from. Each component
is a hi-fi separate in its
own right. And you can
choose from a range of
components all of which
can be controlled by a
single remote. They look
gorgeous in a champagne
metal finish and they
sound sensational.

But beware, once you've
heard them you'll
probably want all three.

Visit your TEAC Stockist for a
demonstration or call TEAC
on 01923 819630
for more information.

Systems!

THE REFERENCE SERIES
Mini & Micro Systems

TEAC WARNING: DUE TO TECHNICAL DIFFICULTIES BEYOND THEIR CONTROL, NO OTHER MINI
OR MICRO SYSTEM WILL BE ABLE TO DELIVER THIS LEVEL OF PERFORMANCE
Chief Musical Officers' Warning

What messages do adverts give us?

Advertisements use powerful images to sell their products. These images contain all sorts of hidden messages about how we should look and dress.

Look at the messages in the advert below.

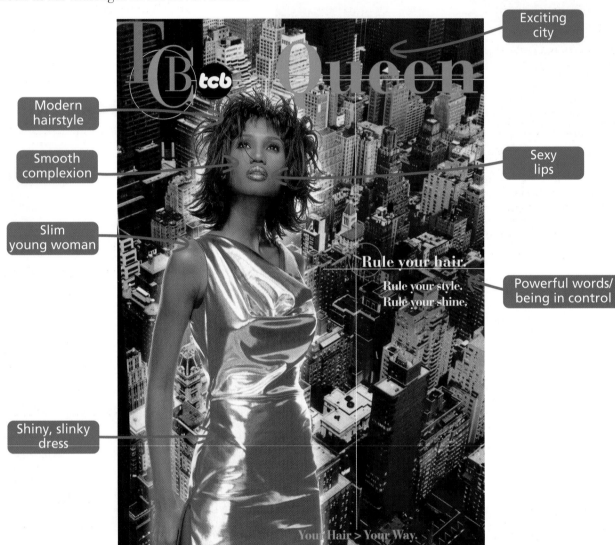

Exciting city

Modern hairstyle

Smooth complexion

Slim young woman

Shiny, slinky dress

Sexy lips

Powerful words/ being in control

Rule your hair.

Rule your style.
Rule your shine.

Your Hair > Your Way.

Activity

Find an advert in a magazine. Cut it out and stick it on a large sheet of white paper. Decide in your group what the words and images suggest. Write notes about the words and images and draw arrows to different parts of the advert, as in the example. Then make a class display.

Discuss

1 Most of us will never look anything like the people in these advertisements, so why do advertisers use them?
2 How do you think the images might affect the way people think about themselves? Is this important or unimportant?

5.3 Can you trust a newspaper?

Fact and opinion

Newspapers bring us the news. Every day we can read about what has happened at home and abroad. We can find out the facts. But newspapers give us more than the facts. Newspaper stories usually give us opinions as well. Different newspapers have different opinions.

A fact is something that can be proved to be true or false. An opinion is what somebody thinks about an issue.

		Fact	Opinion	It depends
a)	The Prime Minister answered questions at 3 o'clock precisely.			
b)	The Prime Minister did not give a clear answer to the first question.			
c)	Spain is a beautiful country.			
d)	Over 3 million people visited Spain last year.			
e)	Wesley weighs 82 kilograms.			
f)	Wesley is fat.			
g)	Wesley would be healthier if he lost weight.			
h)	Gita has been invited to a party on Saturday.			
i)	Gita bought a stunning dress to wear to the party.			
j)	French food is the best in the world.			
k)	Paris is the capital of France.			
l)	It is against the law for anyone under the age of 16 to buy cigarettes.			
m)	Smoking is a dirty habit.			
n)	Smoking can damage your health.			
o)	The car crash killed three people.			
p)	The driver was exceeding the speed limit.			
q)	The driver was driving carelessly.			
r)	Jane and her friend went to see a film.			
s)	The film was a love story.			
t)	The acting in the film was terrible.			

Discuss

As a whole class, discuss why some statements were difficult to categorise as fact or opinion.

How words carry messages

We use words to describe events, explain our feelings, criticise people, praise people, tell a story, give evidence, and so on. We sometimes choose words that express an opinion as well as describe something.

Newspaper headlines and stories

Headline writers in newspapers often choose words that express an opinion rather than simply describe an event.

For example, this is a factual statement –

BOY'S BICYCLE IS STOLEN

It can be written in such a way that the boy is at fault –

FOOLISH BOY LEAVES BICYCLE UNATTENDED

Or it can take the side of the boy –

BIRTHDAY BOY LOSES BIKE TO MEAN THIEVES

1 Look at the words in the box. Which ones are opinion words? Write a list of these.

scoundrel	mean	bubbly	super	upright	person	kind
hateful	schoolgirl	shopper	happy	lively	terrorist	brave
son	fat	mother	foolish	driving	cigarette	worker	steal
soldier	beautiful					

2 Rewrite each of the following statements twice to express different opinions each time.

   a) Girl fails exam
   b) Teacher loses job
   c) Grandmother lives alone
   d) TV star loses weight

3 Read the article on page 85, which appeared in the *Sun* on 29 March 2000.
   a) What is the story about?
   b) On a photocopy of the article, which your teacher will give you, mark all the statements of fact with a blue pen.
   c) On the same photocopy, mark all the opinions with a red pen.
   d) Who seems to be right in the story and who seems to be wrong?
   e) What words suggest which side the writer is on?
   f) What do you think is the opinion of the writer of the story?
   g) Do you agree with this opinion?
   h) Does the story give all the facts?

4 a) Find a story in a recent newspaper. Answer the same questions a)–h) about that story as you did about the 'Dog kicker'.
   b) Find two newspapers that have covered the same story on the same day. Using questions a)–h) compare the facts and opinions in each story. How are they different? Draw a chart like the one below to record your answers.

Question	Newspaper 1	Newspaper 2
What is the story about?		

EXCLUSIVE

By JOHN TROUP

Dog kicker in a dog collar

PET-loving Jean Wood told of her shock yesterday at seeing her playful spaniel viciously kicked in the head – then realising the culprit was wearing a dog collar.

Jean, 55 – whose beloved pooch Bassett had wandered from her garden – said: "Suddenly the man lifted his foot.

"He kicked Bassett hard and deliberately on the head. You could hear a sickening crack as Bassett yelped.

"I couldn't believe my eyes when I looked up at the man and noticed he was wearing a dog collar. He just walked off as if nothing had happened."

Ten-year-old Bassett fled home in agony in Leverington, near Wisbech, Cambs.

Rev Graham Waring, 62, was later arrested by cops who cautioned him for cruelty. Last night he insisted he only "waved" his foot at the King Charles Cavalier.

He said: "I never intended to harm the dog."

But Jean said: "The vet said Bassett was badly bruised. He spent the next 24 hours whimpering in the house.

"I can't understand how a man who purports to be a Christian can be so evil towards an animal."

Angry

Jean told how she and husband Raymond, 70, were in their garden chatting with friends when their dog scampered off. She said:

❛We noticed he had wandered on to the path to say hello to a man who was walking past. Bassett's a friendly little fellow.

Although we don't let him run loose he is allowed out when we are in the garden.

It was obvious from the man's body language he didn't want to stroke him. I guessed he might not like dogs so I went over to pick Bassett up.❜

All creatures great and small . . . Jean, Ray and pet Bassett

Furious Jean claimed the passing priest lashed out with his foot. She said: "I shouted after him that if he was supposed to be a man of God then God help us all."

Husband Raymond said: "I was so angry I rang the RSPCA who advised me to call the police."

An officer took statements from the couple and their friends. Rev Waring was asked to report to Wisbech police station next day.

The priest, who works as a non-stipendiary Church of England minister, arrived with his lawyer and local vicar Francis Wolley.

Rev Waring was immediately arrested. He was taken to nearby March police station where he was cautioned. Last night he said: "The dog began barking loudly and bounding towards me. I instinctively waved my right leg behind me to keep it away. I had no intention of making contact."

The priest – minister for the parishes of Murrow, Southea and Parson Drove – said he had paid the £14.97 vet's bill.

He also informed his archdeacon who had given "nothing but total support and sympathy". But Jean said: "Rev Waring hasn't contacted us to apologise.

"I've always regarded myself as having faith but since this incident I feel some of that faith has gone. It feels horrible."

The RSPCA said: "It is always distressing when someone displays this sort of aggression towards an animal."

5.4 Can you trust a photograph?

Newspaper stories often use photographs to make them more interesting. However, the choice of photograph can influence how the reader thinks about the story. Photographs are very powerful images. People tend to believe photographs.

All sorts of factors affect how a photograph puts across a particular message:

* what the photographer decides to show in the photograph
* what the people in the photograph were doing at the moment the photograph was taken
* the way the people in the photograph have been asked to pose
* the caption that is written to explain it
* the part of the photograph we are allowed to see
* what is in the background of the photograph.

Discuss

Look at Photographs A and B. They were both taken at the same event.

1 How do the different photographs affect our view of the event?
2 Which photograph do you think a newspaper would choose to print to illustrate their coverage of the story, and what caption might they write to go with it?
3 Why do you think one of the photos would be chosen in preference to the other?

Here is a photograph that you haven't seen before. Write a caption that explains what you think is happening in the photograph.

D

Schoolgirls and their parents under police protection as they make their way to Holy Cross Catholic primary school in Belfast. The police are defending them against Protestant protesters who do not want Catholic children going to school in a Protestant area.

Here you can see the full photograph from which Source C on page 87 was taken. It is only when you see the whole image that you can understand what is going on. Cutting bits of a photograph out is called 'cropping' the photograph. This happens frequently in newspapers, books and magazines. Sometimes people crop something if it is blurred or because they want to focus on one part of the photo so it can be seen more clearly. But sometimes it is because they want to put across a particular message or impression.

Discuss

1 Look at the caption you wrote for Photo C on page 87. How does the impression you get change when you see the whole image in Photo D?
2 Make a class list of reasons why people might want to crop photographs, e.g. someone putting together a holiday brochure might want to crop a photograph of a hotel they are advertising because the full photograph shows that there is a rubbish tip next to the hotel.

Activity

Working in pairs or small groups, look through a collection of magazines. Cut out a photograph that you can crop to either: a) change the impression or message it gives you, *or* b) emphasise one section of the photograph, using it in a different way or for a different reason from the original photograph.

Make a copy of the photograph, then crop it and stick both versions on to a piece of paper. Write a new caption for the cropped version.

You could do this for two or three photographs. These could be mounted to form a class display.

Using computers to change photographs

It is getting easier to change photographs. You can scan a photograph into a computer and then alter it, for instance:

* if one person in a group looks miserable, you can crop out the head and replace it with one from another scanned photo where the same person is smiling
* you can make people look more attractive by 'airbrushing' (removing) the bits that don't look so good
* you can change the background of the photograph and give it a completely different setting.

Discuss

1 Look at Photo E. If you were a holiday company wanting to attract people to this place, how might you change this photograph? What would you take out and what might you put in? Write a caption for the new photograph.
2 If you were a campaigner against noise pollution, how might you use this photograph? Write a caption for it.
3 After working through pages 86–89, discuss why you cannot always trust the photographs that you see in newspapers, books or magazines.

The weekly Air France flight lands at St Martin

Activity

1 Take your own photographs to put across a particular message.
   You could do this for your school or the area around your school. You could create a good image or a bad image, perhaps using the suggestions on the right.
2 Write captions for your photos and then mount them on a display.

Good image
* School – photos of pupils working, new gymnasium, smiling headteacher talking to pupils.
* Local area – library, new buildings, smiling shopkeeper outside shop.

Bad image
* School – toilets, graffiti, broken furniture, noisy class.
* Local area – rubbish on streets, boarded-up shop, shopkeeper shouting at young person.

As a member of the United Council for Galactic Trade's team of investigators you have already visited Planet Hoff in sections 1, 2 and 4 (see pages 2–3, 18–19 and 62–63). This time your team of investigators is looking at all forms of media on Hoff. They want to find out if the media on Hoff follows the intergalactic agreement on press and broadcasting freedom, shown in the box on the right. You can find a description of the different groups who live on the planet on pages 18–19.

Activity

Read the box on freedom of press (newspapers) and broadcasting (radio and television) on the right.

1 **Are the news sheets on Hoff free to print whatever they like?**
2 **Can the television programmes broadcast what they like?**
3 **In what ways are the Uppers and Thinkers who control the media breaking the intergalactic agreement on press and broadcasting freedom?**
4 **How do you think the media on Hoff will have to change?**

Press and broadcasting freedom

- A society should allow all views to be published or heard, unless they incite violence or racial hatred.
- The media should be owned by a variety of people in order to give a range of views.
- The people who work in the media should not be influenced by the government or by the people who own the media.
- The media should be free to report on things that the public needs to know.
- People should be able to complain if the media have told lies about them.

MEDIA ZONE

HOFF Media 5

The media on Planet Hoff

The television stations on Hoff are run by the Thinkers. They are the educated members of the society, so they produce the programmes and broadcast them. The Thinkers also write the daily electronic news sheets, which people can receive on their television sets. Capitos and Doers are not allowed to make programmes or write news sheets. All homes in Hoff have televisions, except the homes of most Gronks. They are too poor to have television, but they can watch it in bars and libraries.

Before any television programme or electronic news sheet can be broadcast, a special committee of Thinkers has to look at it and decide whether it is acceptable for broadcast. The rules have been agreed with the Uppers and are quite strict. They say that programmes and news sheets should:

* not criticise the Uppers or the Sesar
* not suggest any changes to the way of life on Hoff
* never use swear words or offensive images
* only use news stories that have been agreed with Uppers
* make the inhabitants feel good about their lives and so they should not show or describe bad aspects of Hoff.

Any programme or news sheet that breaks these rules cannot be broadcast. In some cases, the programme-maker could be arrested. In the past there have been cases of Thinkers being put in prison for making programmes critical of Hoff.

You can find out more about Planet Hoff on pages 2–3, 18–19 and 62–63.

Freedom of the press

1 In this country, people disagree about whether newspapers have too much or not enough freedom. The pictures below show different points of view about press freedom. Match each picture with one of the statements about press freedom.

D

A

B

It's all lies! I'm ruined!

C

Statements

1 Newspapers dig into people's private lives and print things that cause a lot of damage.

2 We need newspapers to find out the truth, otherwise rich and powerful people could get away with wrongdoing.

3 The people have a right to know about matters that affect everyone.

4 Newspapers exaggerate or even tell lies to sell copies. They don't care if what they say is not true.

5 Famous people should expect others to be interested in their private lives. It's the price you pay for fame and fortune.

6 Newspaper journalists hound people to get stories.

7 The laws of libel in this country are strong enough to protect people. You can always sue in court.

8 Sometimes newspapers can affect the outcome of a trial because they print information that could influence a jury.

E

My client's reputation has been ruined and we demand compensation.

F

Our sales are down. We need a juicy story.

G

I know he did it. I read all about him in the papers!

H

Discuss

1 a) Which of the statements argue *for* press freedom?
   b) Which ones argue for more control of the press?
   c) Which statements do you agree with?
2 Hold a class debate on whether you think the press should be more controlled or have more freedom.
3 Planet Hoff shows us that the media can be controlled by governments so that we only find out what they want us to know. There are plenty of examples of this happening on our own planet in recent times. Why is it important that governments don't control what we read in the papers, see on television or hear on the radio?

5.6 The media and their controls

Press

The press includes newspapers and magazines.
Newspapers are daily or weekly. They can be split into:

* **tabloids** – smaller papers like the *Sun* and the *Mirror*, which are easy to read but do not provide very much news. They usually have wide coverage of sport, stories relating to television personalities or celebrities, and stories of a more personal nature.
* **broadsheets** – large papers like *The Times* and the *Guardian*, which contain more serious news stories and coverage of world events.

There are a huge number of different magazines, which tend to come out weekly or monthly.

The Press Complaints Commission makes sure that newspapers and magazines follow a code of practice. This says that they should not publish inaccurate or misleading stories. They should also respect an individual's privacy (unless there is a public interest in something they have done) and not harass people. The Commission also looks into complaints.

Television

There are terrestrial channels, such as the BBC and ITV1 (independent television), and satellite channels such as Sky. Television can also be provided by way of cables. The newest development is digital television, which allows viewers to receive many more channels on their television sets.

The BBC has regulations to control its standards. It says that its programmes should be accurate, truthful, balanced and fair to the people who take part. It has rules for dealing with complaints. Independent television is regulated by the Independent Television Commission (ITC). It looks after viewers' interests by setting standards for programmes and advertising.

Advertising

Advertisements can be found in a variety of forms on television and radio, in the cinema, on posters, on buildings, at sports events and in many other places.

The Advertising Standards Authority (ASA) was set up in 1962 to make sure that advertisements in the UK are legal, decent, honest and truthful. It handles complaints and can insist that adverts are withdrawn immediately.

Cinema

In Britain the British Board of Film Censors gives each new film a certificate rating, as below:

* U – suitable for everybody
* PG – parental guidance, when an adult has to accompany a child under 12
* 12 – for 12-year-olds and over
* 15 – for 15-year-olds and over
* 18 – for 18-year-olds and over.

If the censors regard a film as unsuitable, they can ask for bits to be cut out or they can refuse to give a film a certificate rating which means it cannot be shown in cinemas at all.

The internet

A widely used form of media is the internet. This is a source of information on a limitless number of topics. It is also used increasingly to sell goods and services to users. The internet is not regulated.

Channel	Average viewing weekly (hrs:mins per person)	Share of total viewing (%)
All TV	24:05	100.0
BBC1	6:20	26.3
BBC2	2:32	10.2
ITV1	6:51	28.5
Channel 4/S4C	2:51	11.8
Channel 5	1:21	5.6
Other viewing	4:10	17.3

**Hours of viewing and share of audience
Week ending 10 September 2000**

section 6

Global citizenship
What part do you play in the world?

Key words
- migrant
- refugee
- asylum seeker
- global
- charity
- human rights

People all over the world depend upon each other. We say, 'the world is shrinking' because it is easy now to communicate with people instantly via telephones, e-mail and faxes across very large distances. It is also quick to travel anywhere in the world. People travel to different countries for holidays, on business, to visit relatives, to work and to live. We buy goods that are made abroad and countries often have trading agreements.

But there are still wars between countries and civil wars between different groups within countries. These cause death, distress and acts of inhumanity. There are millions of refugees in the world as a result of such conflict. There are also natural disasters, like floods and volcanoes, which cause great suffering and distress. When a disaster happens somewhere in the world, other countries send help – money, food, clothes, medicines, experts.

In this section, you will learn about:

* the ideas we have about other countries
* how our ideas are shaped by images in the media
* how charities help people in countries throughout the world
* reasons for helping people in other countries
* aid programmes.

You will:

* think about moral issues and decide what is right
* discuss these issues in small groups and as a whole class
* use your imagination to consider other people's experiences
* take part in a class project to raise money for an appeal.

What do you know about other countries?

We all have ideas in our head about what other countries are like. Many of us have friends and relatives who have lived in or were born in other countries. Some of us were born abroad ourselves. Lots of people from this country go on holidays to places in different parts of the world.

Activity

You need a blank world map and an atlas. Work in groups of four or five.

1 Talk in your group and list all the countries where someone in the group has relatives living. Mark these countries with a red cross.

2 Now list all the countries that you have visited, whether on holiday or to visit relatives, or where you have lived. Mark these countries with a blue cross.

3 How many countries have you marked? List them all. Write them all up on a large sheet of paper. When all groups have done this, see how many countries appear on the list.

Discuss

1 Brainstorm the images you have of the following countries and the people who live there: Italy, the United States, Ethiopia, India and China.

2 Has anyone in the class been to any of these countries? If so, do they agree with the images?

3 Where do we get our images of other countries from?

Rich and poor

When people talk about the world as a whole, they like to divide it up into 'rich' countries and 'poor' countries. Rich countries are likely to be in Europe, North America, Australia and parts of Asia. Poor countries are likely to be in Africa, Asia and Latin America. However, this division is too simple. Not everybody in a rich country is rich, and not everybody in a poor country is poor. There is poverty in rich countries and wealth in poorer countries.

People also use other names to describe the division between countries. The table on the right gives examples.

The reason why people use these other names is because they don't want to suggest that

Rich	Poor
Developed	Developing or underdeveloped
First World	Third World or Majority World
North	South
More Economically Developed Country (MEDC)	Less Economically Developed Country (LEDC)

everything about richer countries is better than everything about poorer ones. Richer countries have problems too, such as pollution, crime, homelessness and unemployment. Some poorer countries have a quality of life based on their families and communities that people in richer countries envy. The problem is that when we hear about people in poorer countries, it is usually when they have been affected by some sort of disaster. This gives the impression that nothing else happens in these countries.

Images of developing countries

What images do you have of other countries referred to as Third World or developing countries?

On these two pages you can see two collections of images: Collection A and Collection B.

Collection A

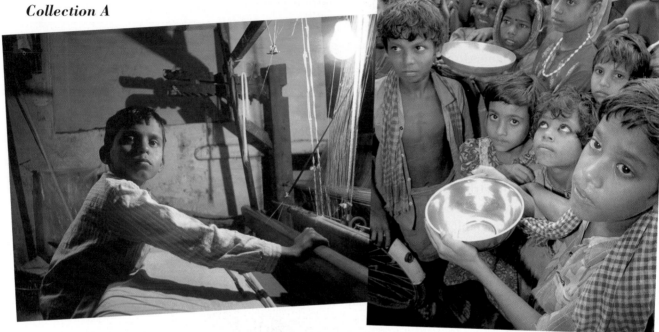

Collection B

Activity

1 Look at Collection A. What ideas about the people from these countries do these pictures give you?
2 Look at Collection B.
   a) What ideas about the people do these pictures suggest?
   b) How are they different from the pictures in Collection A?
3 Which collection is closest to the view that you had formed of developing countries?
4 Why do you think we see so many of the type of images in Collection A in our media and very few of Collection B?
5 How does this affect our views of the people who live in developing countries?

6.2 Refugees and migrants

Why do people move from one country to another?

If we look back into our own histories, we can usually find members of our family who have made a decision to leave their birthplace and seek a better life in another country. People have come to the United Kingdom over centuries to make up the rich and varied population we have today (see page 37). Similarly, many people have left the UK to go and live in other countries, such as Australia, Canada and parts of Africa.

People migrate for many reasons. Usually these reasons are to do with:

* things that cause people to leave their homeland – push factors
* things that attract people to new countries – pull factors.

People do not usually move for just one reason. The decision to migrate is taken for a variety of 'push' and 'pull' reasons.

Activity

1 Decide which of the factors below are push factors and which are pull factors. Complete your own copy of the following chart.

Push	Pull

a) High unemployment
b) People needed to do jobs
c) Civil war
d) Better education
e) People can say what they like without fear of imprisonment
f) Fear of being persecuted because of religion
g) Fear of imprisonment and torture because of political views
h) Hunger
i) Better-paid jobs
j) Safety, strong system of law and order
k) Enough food and water for everybody
l) Better housing
m) Fear of attack because of ethnic group
n) Poverty, little chance to make a good living
o) Overcrowding, not enough land to go around
p) War with a neighbouring country
q) Freedom of expression and movement

2 Match speech bubbles A–H with one of the push/pull factors in your lists: for example, B = civil war.

A I had heard that the government of this country wanted people to come and work in certain jobs, as there were not enough people to do them.

B There has been a war going on in my country for ten years. Nobody is safe and there is no chance of building a decent life for my family.

C I was forced to join the army at the age of thirteen to fight for our country. I am now fourteen and I am frightened that I am going to be killed.

D I was against the government and said so in public. I was beaten and threatened that I would be tortured or killed if I spoke out again.

Why do people become refugees?

Many people do not have a choice about whether they leave their country to live somewhere else. Throughout history, families have been forced to flee their homes because they have been victimised and made to fear for their lives. The Pilgrim Fathers fled to America in the seventeenth century to escape persecution. In the nineteenth century, Jews were forced to flee from Russia and eastern Europe because their homes were being attacked. In the twentieth century, two world wars led to millions of people being left without a home as they were pushed out of land they had once lived in. The reasons that have caused people to flee – to become refugees – are often the same in history: war, persecution and intolerance.

After the Second World War, the United Nations (UN) was determined to do something about the plight of refugees. In 1951 a special UN Convention encouraged countries to work together to try to protect the human rights of refugees and to solve their problems by helping them return to their own country or, if they were still threatened, to settle somewhere else.

There were hopes that the refugee problem would get better, but in the last 40 years the situation has not improved. Civil wars, brutal governments and fighting between different ethnic groups have led to the same old story of violence and persecution. There are millions of refugees living in developing countries that are themselves poor. A few find refuge in richer countries, where they settle into new lives with homes and jobs.

E Our relatives say the country is very wealthy and, if you work hard, you can be successful.

F In this country you are free to say what you like and go where you like.

G The soldiers beat me and my daughters because of our religion. We couldn't bear it any more.

H I am a trained doctor but there are no jobs here. I want to live somewhere where I could work and earn a better living for my family.

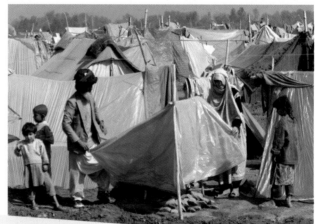

An Afghan family in a refugee camp in Pakistan, March 2001

Who is a refugee?

Refugees are people who flee their country because of a well-founded fear of persecution for reasons of race, religion, nationality, political opinion or membership of a particular social group. A refugee either cannot return home or is afraid to do so. (Definition from the United Nations High Commission on Refugees, UNHCR)

People tend to think of refugees in large numbers, but they are all individuals with their own stories to tell, as you can see in the case studies below and on page 103.

Discuss

Look at the three case studies and discuss:

1 **What sorts of events cause people to flee their country?**
2 **What experiences do you think they might have had during their flight to safety?**
3 **The United Nations has drawn up a Universal Declaration of Human Rights (see page 112). Which of these rights have been abused or denied in the case studies?**

Case study 1: Maria's story

'I am seventeen and a half. I come from Kosovo where they have massacred so many women and children. I had to leave because they tortured my father-in-law. He begged me to save my daughter. I didn't have anything to pack because they burnt my house down. I had to borrow some clothes to start the journey. We travelled for six days. It was terrible being in a lorry. It was very cold. My husband is dead. He stepped on a landmine. I received the news by fax. I lost all hope.'

Case study 2: Mohamad's story

Mohamad comes from Sri Lanka. He is 22 years old. A gentle, soft-spoken, religious young man, he has been imprisoned in three different countries. He is a Tamil who was caught up in the fierce fighting between the Sri Lankan government and the Tamil Tigers, a group who are rebelling against the government. Mohamad's brother was killed by the Tigers and they approached Mohamad several times to demand that he get supplies such as oil and batteries for them. He was also arrested and tortured by government forces who accused him of helping the Tigers. 'They hung me upside down and beat me with a pipe,' he said. He is still unable to move his left arm properly.

Trapped in the middle of the fighting, he realised that he would be killed by the Tigers if he did not escape. So his father paid someone to take Mohamad to Germany where he believed he would be safe. After a long and difficult journey he arrived on the German border where he was arrested. 'They put me in a dark room. I was very afraid that they would send me back to Sri Lanka.' Later he was taken to prison where he shared a cell with common criminals and, not knowing any German, he remained in virtual silence.

A German court ruled that he had entered Germany illegally and would be deported because Germany does not consider that people fleeing from non-governmental groups like the Tamil Tigers are refugees. However, he was allowed to stay in Germany and was sent to a camp in East Germany. There he was treated very badly and became the victim of racist attacks. The local people beat him up and spat on him in the street. Mohamad was bitter about his treatment: 'I hated that place. The people were very harsh,' he said.

In desperation, he made his way to the UK and claimed asylum. He stayed with Tamil acquaintances while his claim was processed. 'I was very happy in London', he said. But then he was told that he had to go back to Germany as that was the first safe country he had stayed in. Mohamad argued that if he was sent back to Germany he would be deported to Sri Lanka, where he would almost certainly be killed. But he was ignored. He is appealing against the order to send him back to Germany.

Case study 3: Jacob's story

Jacob had dreamed of living in a place where there was no fighting

" In my home town in the southern Sudan, there was fighting everywhere. Everyone was running from the bombs. Even our goats were bombed. No one had time to plant the crops. So I just left.

There were so many people walking on the road. I had nothing. No clothes. No food. The first day I didn't eat. I just ran. The first night I remembered the wild animals I had seen along the road. I was afraid, so I climbed up a tree to sleep. But I couldn't sleep. I thought that something would come and pull me down. "

Jacob joined up with many others on the road

" One day we came to a place that had mines. Someone was blown up and everyone started running and there was blood everywhere. We held hands tightly and ran across the field. We walked and walked. We saw villages where there was nobody, not even a cat. We had no food and people started eating leaves. After ten days people in our group began to die. One night an old man said he could not walk any more. An hour later he died. We crossed a river and planes dropped bombs on us. I was very tired but we reached the [refugee] camp in Ethiopia. There are many people here from Sudan just like me. Now I go to school again. In the camp there is food and medicine. The sound of planes no longer frightens me because I know they are carrying food not bombs. This is the place I dreamed of. "

Source: Adapted from *Refugee Children* (Geneva UNHCR)

Activity

What would be the main problems facing a family of refugees in a foreign country? Some have been suggested on the diagram below.

a) Explain each of these from the point of view of the refugees. Here is an example:

WORK – I need to find a job to support my family. Is it possible to use the skills I already have? Does this country recognise my qualifications or do I have to start from the bottom?

b) What other problems do you think a refugee might face?

c) Discuss how we can help refugees coming to our country or to our school.

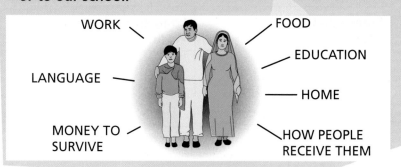

WORK · FOOD
EDUCATION
LANGUAGE
HOME
MONEY TO SURVIVE
HOW PEOPLE RECEIVE THEM

6.3 How do charities try to help?

You will be familiar with appeals made by charities for money to help people in other countries. These often occur after disasters caused by floods, earthquakes or volcanoes, or by the climate when a country has a long period of drought. Often these countries were quite prosperous until the disaster struck and they need help to get them through a difficult time.

But this is often only a small part of the work that charities do in developing countries. Much of their work is concerned with longer-term projects to help the people help themselves.

Activity

Look at these pictures, which show some of the different things that charities do. They can be grouped into two sections:

- work that charities do to help in emergencies and disasters
- long-term development work designed to help people to help themselves.

Decide which category you would put each type of work in, and complete the following chart.

Emergencies and disasters	Long-term development work

Books

Wells

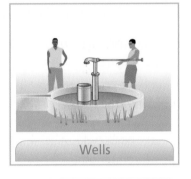

Computers

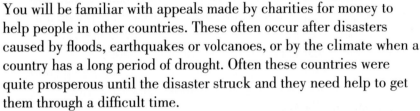

Medical supplies

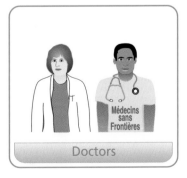

Doctors

Food

Seeds

Hospitals

Tools

Blankets and clothing

Tents

Fresh water supplies

Teachers

Irrigation

Tractors

Discuss

1 How did you decide which types of aid went in the emergencies and disasters column?

2 What do the types of aid that you put in the long-term column suggest about the other work that charities do?

3 Why do you think we mainly hear about charities during disasters?

4 Do you think charities use the images of children suffering in disasters in order to raise more money for their work?

5 Do you think it is right that charities use these images?

Should you help?

Most people support charities and the work they do in developing countries. But some people argue that it is not always a good idea to give lots of money to charities. Some of the reasons they give are shown below together with some of the reasons for supporting charities. What do you think?

Discuss

1 Look at the following statements about whether we should help countries affected by disasters and longer-term problems. Decide whether you agree or disagree with each statement.

2 After you have done this, discuss each of the statements as a whole class. Are there any other reasons that you can think of why we should or should not help? Add these to the discussion.

A We should always help people worse off than ourselves. It is morally the right thing to do.

B If we don't help people in trouble, others might not help us when we are in need.

C Other people's problems are nothing to do with me. I have enough problems of my own.

D How can anyone see pictures of human suffering and not help? Especially when it's children.

E Helping people in poor countries makes them dependent on aid. We should encourage them to help themselves.

F It's good to help less fortunate people because it helps us to count our own blessings and be thankful.

G The real problem is over-population. People in poor countries should have smaller families.

H Poor countries are poor because of the way rich people treated them in the past. We owe it to poor countries to help them.

I Money that I give to charity might end up in the pocket of someone dishonest, not helping people in need.

J We should help poor people in this country before giving money for other countries.

K It's a religious duty to help people wherever they live.

Charities at work

A great deal of the aid that goes to poorer countries in the world is organised by charities such as Oxfam, Christian Aid, the Red Cross and Muslim Aid. They often work with governments and the United Nations to help communities that are in distress. They collect a huge amount of money to spend on a variety of projects.

Discuss

1 a) What sorts of things would you miss most if you did not have them at home? Name three things but don't include people.

b) What things would you be unable to do if you did not have electricity in your house?

c) What problems would occur if the water was switched off for a day in your house?

d) Under what circumstances might it happen that we did not have water and electricity? What would our lives be like?

e) What do you think is the difference between things that we want and things that we need?

2 a) Do you think that the Ten Basic Rights on the pamphlet shown here are needs or wants?

b) Why are the Ten Basic Rights so important for people throughout the world?

c) Would you give up some of your wants so that other people could have their needs met?

3 Of the Ten Basic Rights, which three do you think charities should concentrate most on helping to provide?

Every person has a BASIC RIGHT to:

Enough to eat
Denied:
800 million people go hungry.

But possible:
"We've grown sorghum here since 1985. We've had a harvest every year – it's never failed, even during the drought years."
Arakudi Apalia Lobe, Kenya, working successfully with a food and farming project.

Clean water
Denied:
More than a billion people are at risk from dirty water. 25,000 die each day.

But possible:
"Before we had to get water from a pool 2km away. The water was dirty and lots of us got ill. Now the health of the people here is better."
Oun Svey's village in Cambodia now has 11 wells, funded by Oxfam, built by the villagers.

A livelihood
Denied:
One in four of the world's people lives in abject poverty.

But possible:
Fair trade, with fair prices, makes sure that the people who grow our coffee, make chocolate and produce handcrafts, don't have to live in poverty. Oxfam campaigners – people like you – have made this principle work. Because of these efforts, we can buy Fair Trade coffee, chocolate and tea in all major supermarkets. Because of these efforts, producers can send their children to school, and can afford enough to eat.

A home
Denied:
Millions of children live on the streets of the world's cities.

But possible:
Vinod used to live on the street in Mysore, India. He's twelve, but has lived a life of danger and neglect. Oxfam funds a shelter which gives Vinod a bed, a place to play and some schooling.

An education
Denied:
31% of people in the third world are illiterate.

But possible:
Macuxi Indians in the far north of the Brazilian Amazon had no school. The education system did not recognise their language or their culture. They've built their own school, and written their own textbooks in the Macuxi language.

Health care
Denied:
10% of children in the third world die before the age of five.

But possible:
At Ibanda health centre in Uganda, children are immunised against killer diseases.

A safe environment
Denied:
Pollution and environmental disaster threaten millions of the world's poorest people.

But possible:
In the Ky Anh district of Vietnam, land is regularly flooded by the sea. Villagers have built dykes, and now, as extra protection, village women have planted mangrove trees. More planting is planned.

Protection from violence
Denied:
90% of war casualties are civilians. 100 million landmines lie waiting.

But possible:
Oxfam, with other organisations, is campaigning for a total ban on mines. And in Angola, where between eight and 20 million mines are maiming and killing, Oxfam has funded mine-clearance operations.

Equality of opportunity
Denied:
For reasons of race, sex, religion or nationality, people are exploited or ignored.

But possible:
Women of the Untouchable caste in Bihar, India have been able to question for the first time their lives of service and poverty. An Oxfam-supported project gives education and a confidence the women have never had.

A say in their future
Denied:
Poor people are the last to be heard and the first to suffer.

But possible:
"I say to people: instead of coming to my door all steamed up, why don't we go all together to the door of the government!"
Ivanete Paulino Tavares, leader of a residents' campaign for services in the shanty town of Alto dos Milagres, Recife, Brazil.

An extract from an Oxfam campaign leaflet showing ten things that all people have a right to and should be able to expect.

What do the charities spend their money on?

1 *Helping the victims of natural disasters*

When disasters such as flood, famine and earthquakes hit, charities send food, medicine and clothing. They help people to find temporary homes and receive clean water supplies, so as to prevent the spread of diseases like typhoid and dysentery.

Charities spend their money on three main areas.

2 *Development work*

Charities work on longer-term projects to make people less dependent on help from outside. These might be to develop skills in literacy and typing, crafts like carpentry or in computers and electronics. They might be projects like the ones described in the WaterAid case study on page 109.

3 *Campaigns*

Charities mount campaigns for human rights in various countries. Some charities argue that the richer countries cause some of the problems of people living in developing countries. The 'Fair Trade' campaign encourages people in richer countries to pay a reasonable price for goods such as coffee and rugs, and make sure the people who grow or produce the products get the money.

Discuss

1 The cartoons above represent four different ways charities work with people. What are they?
2 Which ways are most like the ways WaterAid works?
3 What is the value of long-term development work?
4 How do the WaterAid projects benefit the communities they work with?
5 Do you think it is important to get the people in local communities involved in the projects, or should the work be done for them?
6 Do you think it should be left to charities to provide aid when disasters strike?

Activity

Produce a campaign leaflet for a charity to encourage people to give money. You should explain the aims of the charity and what it is trying to do with the money.

You might find it useful to collect some real charity leaflets to give you ideas.

Case study: WaterAid

WaterAid has a very clear and simple aim – to help all people have access to clean and safe water. This means water for drinking, cooking and washing. Contaminated water is responsible for millions of deaths each year as well as disease and illness, especially among children. WaterAid also helps out with sanitation and hygiene education.

One estimate suggests that safe water and good sanitation cut the number of deaths of children under five years old by over 50 per cent. Children are particularly likely to suffer from lack of water and dirty water. Dirty water causes diarrhoea and dehydration, which can lead to death. Lack of water means that children cannot wash often enough, and this causes skin diseases and eye infections.

A mother in Tanzania explains:

> In the dry season I shut my children in the house during the hottest time of the day. If they play outside, they sweat too much and I do not have enough water for them to drink to replace the sweat.

What does WaterAid do?

WaterAid works with local organisations and local communities. The local people themselves work on the project so they feel it is their achievement. Also it means they do not depend on the charity over a long period. The projects include:

- setting up a system of pipes to carry clean water to villages. Some people, often women and children, have to travel hours to get water. Water is very heavy and can damage people's necks and backs.
- digging wells
- educating children in good hygiene practices that they will pass on to their families.

Samuel Dugbate, a 27-year-old farmer in Ghana, says:

> I decided to take an active part in the construction of the well because I realised that the stream from which we fetch water makes us ill. We are all eager about the well and therefore do not find the work difficult.

h₂op to it!

25 great fundraising ideas

WaterAid is the UK's only major charity which is dedicated to the provision of safe domestic water, sanitation and hygiene promotion to the world's poorest people. If you would like to support **WaterAid**'s vital work please read on for some great fundraising ideas...

WaterAid
www.wateraid.org.uk

Plan a campaign

Charities don't simply collect money after disasters have happened. You have found out about some of the long-term development work of charities. As a class, you may have made contact with or adopted a particular charity. Some schools have their own 'pet charities'.

As a class, decide which charity you would like to work more closely with. Find out what it does.

- Collect information about the charity. You could write letters, telephone the charity, invite a speaker to the class or visit the charity's website.
- Now plan a campaign to raise people's awareness of the long-term work of the charity. Discuss with the charity workers how you could help.
- Think about all the different ways you can publicise the work of the charity. You should consider posters, leaflets, mailshots, newspaper articles, local radio, petitions, fundraising events, school assemblies, badges, etc.
- Different groups in the class can work on different aspects of the campaign.
  Remember that the main messages to get across are:
  – the aims of the charity
  – the need it is trying to meet
  – how the charity is helping people
  – whom is being helped
  – some examples of success
  – what people can do to help the charity.
- When each group has planned its part of the campaign, prepare a group presentation on how the whole class will run the campaign. You could invite the charity workers in to hear your presentation.

Plan a fundraising event

Comic Relief has encouraged young people to put on special events on 'Red Nose Day' to help people all around the world.

Plan and run a fundraising event for 'Red Nose Day'. Comic Relief produces a pack to help you do this.

Make decisions as a class about the following aspects of the event:

- What will the event be?
- How will you arrange sponsorship?
- Who will keep track of the money?
- Where will it be kept?
- Who will be responsible for sending it off to Comic Relief?

6.4 Organisations that help the world

When people in the world are suffering from wars, disasters, floods, diseases and political or religious oppression, there are organisations that try to help. Some of these are set up and paid for by the governments of different countries which have agreed to work together. Most of their work is done through the United Nations.

United Nations (UN)

The United Nations was set up in 1945 in San Francisco at the end of the Second World War when 51 nations signed the UN Charter (its rules). The horrors of the war and the problems it created made the leaders of countries throughout the world realise that there had to be a better way of settling arguments between countries. Millions of people had lost their lives in the war; millions had been made refugees; hundreds of thousands of children had lost their parents; many countries were suffering from poverty and disease. These problems have continued and the UN has not been able to stop wars, but it is still dedicated to helping people in distress where it can.

The flag of the United Nations shows two olive branches (symbols of peace) embracing the world.

The aims of the UN are to:

* prevent wars wherever possible
* develop friendly relations between countries
* get international co-operation in solving international problems, such as refugees
* get all countries to respect basic human rights
* achieve freedoms for all, whatever their race, sex, language or religion.

Work being carried out by UN organisations

Most countries in the world now support the United Nations. The UN runs several organisations designed to help people throughout the world. For example, the World Health Organization (WHO) tries to improve the health of people in all countries and fight diseases by vaccination programmes.

The UN refugee organisation, UNHCR, safeguards the rights and well-being of refugees. It tries to assist refugees to return to their own countries, or, if this is impossible, resettles them in safety in another country.

The United Nations Children's Fund, UNICEF, works with governments to ensure that the most needy children are immunised, have health care, clean water and nutritious food, and go to school. UNICEF helps families with children in times of conflict or disaster.

Part of the UN's Universal Declaration of Human Rights

On 10 December 1948, the United Nations approved the **Universal Declaration of Human Rights**. This document was meant to be a standard by which people could judge whether a government was treating its people properly. Here is a summary of some of the rights set out in the declaration.

1   All human beings are born free and equal in dignity and rights.

2   Everyone is entitled to all the rights and freedoms in this declaration without distinction of any kind, such as race, colour, sex, language, political or other opinion, national or social origin, property, birth or other status.

3   Everyone has the right to life and liberty.

4   No one shall be held in slavery.

5   No one shall be subjected to torture or to cruel, inhuman or degrading treatment or punishment.

6   All are equal before the law.

7   No one shall be subjected to arbitrary (unreasonable) arrest, detention or exile.

8   Everyone is entitled to a fair trial, in public.

9   Everyone accused of a crime in a court of law is presumed innocent until proved guilty in a public trial in which they have a right to defend themselves.

10 No one shall be subjected to interference with their privacy, family, home or correspondence.

11 Everyone has the right of freedom of movement and residence within the borders of each state, and the right to leave and return freely to their country.

12 Everyone has the right to seek asylum from prosecution in other countries.

13 Men and women of full age have the right to marry and found a family without limitation due to race, nationality or religion.

14 Everyone has the right to own property.

15 Everyone has the right to freedom of thought, conscience and religion.

16 Everyone has the right to freedom of opinion and expression.

17 Everyone has the right to meet freely in peaceful organisations.

18 Everyone has the right to take part in the government of their country.

19 Everyone has the right to work, to free choice of employment, and to equal pay for equal work.

20 Everyone has the right to rest and leisure.

21 Everyone has the right to a standard of living adequate for the health and well-being of themselves and their family, including food, clothing, housing and medical care.

22 Everyone has the right to an education. Education shall be free and compulsory.

23 Everyone has the right to take part in the cultural life of the community.

Key words

asylum seeker someone who wants to be regarded as a refugee so that they cannot be forced to return to their country where they may be imprisoned, tortured, killed or suffer some other form of persecution

censorship banning or changing material (newspaper articles, books, films, photographs) to prevent it being seen by the public

charity the giving of help, money or food to those in need, or an organisation set up to provide these things

community a group of people who live near each other in a local area; a group of people who share common beliefs or ways of life

councillor a person who is elected to sit on a council

democracy a system of government where people regularly elect their leaders and have a say in the way a country is governed

discrimination treating someone unfairly because of your prejudices

election a way of choosing someone for a particular position by voting

fact something that can be proved to be true

fairness treating people in a just, unbiased way

global worldwide

government the group of people who run a country

human rights rights that are held to belong to any person. The United Nations Universal Declaration of Human Rights, 1948, sets out a full list of the rights that all people should have. These include the right to life, liberty, education, freedom of movement and equality before the law.

image the way a person, a country, a place or an event is represented: for example, by a picture, a diagram or a description

intolerance refusing to accept that other people have a right to be different; not tolerating other people's views, beliefs and behaviour

media ways of communicating with lots of people: for example, newspapers, television, internet, cinema, books, magazines

Member of Parliament someone who is elected to sit in Parliament to represent the people who voted for them

migrant someone who moves from one place to another, to live and work there

monarchy a system of government in which a king or queen plays an important part in running a country

opinion what somebody thinks about a particular issue; not fact

Parliament the place where people meet to discuss important issues, make laws and question the government about the way it is running the country

policy a course of action that people plan to carry out or are in the process of carrying out

prejudice opinions that we form without knowing all the facts or much information

Prime Minister the leader of the government

punishment a penalty for a crime or offence: for example, school detention, imprisonment

refugee a person who seeks shelter in another country from war, persecution or natural disaster

responsibility recognising what you owe to other people in your community; acting towards other people in a caring or thoughtful way; being accountable for your own actions

rights how a person expects or wants to be treated by others

rules the code of behaviour that is laid down in a group or organisation, which everyone is expected to obey

sanction a punishment to make someone or a group of people do what others want them to do

services jobs done by the local council for the benefit of people living in the area it controls, e.g. running the local library, collecting rubbish, cleaning the streets

stereotype a description of groups of people who have something in common, such as their religion, their age, their sex or their nationality. The description is applied to everyone in the group and ignores individual differences between people

Index